*R*ussia *and the*
*U*SSR 1900-1995

TONY DOWNEY

WITH

NIGEL SMITH

OXFORD
UNIVERSITY PRESS

OXFORD
UNIVERSITY PRESS

Great Clarendon Street, Oxford OX2 6DP

Oxford University Press is a department of the University of Oxford.
It furthers the University's objective of excellence in research, scholarship,
and education by publishing worldwide in

Oxford New York
Athens Auckland Bangkok Bogotá Buenos Aires Calcutta
Cape Town Chennai Dar es Salaam Delhi Florence Hong Kong Istanbul
Karachi Kuala Lumpur Madrid Melbourne Mexico City Mumbai Nairobi
Paris São Paulo Shanghai Singapore Taipei Tokyo Toronto Warsaw

with associated companies in *Berlin Ibadan*

Oxford is a registered trade mark of Oxford University Press
in the UK and in certain other countries

© Oxford University Press 1996

ISBN 0 19 917248 X

Printed in Hong Kong

Acknowledgements

The publishers would like to thank the
following for their permission to reproduce
the following photographs:

Camera Press Ltd: p 77; Corbis UK
Ltd/Bettmann/UPI: pps 73, 79, 85, 93;
Fotomas Index: p 7; Hulton Deutsch
Collection Ltd: pps 12 bottom, 14, 20;
Imperial War Musuem: pps 15, 60 top, 71;
David King Collection: pps 4, 5 top, 6, 9, 11
top, 12 top, 16 left, 18 top, 19, 22, 23, 26, 28,
30, 31, 32, 38, 40, 42 top right & bottom, 43
bottom, 49, 50, 51, 55 bottom, 56, 59, 60
bottom, 61, 63, 64, 65, 76, 84;   The Mansell
Collection Ltd: pps 5 bottom, 13, 16 right;
Network Photographers: p 88; Novosti
(London) Photo Library: pps 8, 18 bottom, 36,
39, 41, 42 top left; Popperfoto: pps 10, 11
bottom, 67, 72, 82, 83, 87, 89; School of
Slavonic Studies/Krokodil: p 78 bottom;
Thames & Hudson: p 34; Topham
Picturepoint: pps 43 top, 78 top, 86, 92;
Topham Picturepoint/Associated Press: pps 90,
94; Centre of the Study of Cartoon &
Caricature/University of Kent: p 69; Centre of
the Study of Cartoon & Caricature/University
of Kent/John Appleton: pps 55 top, 57;

Cover photographs are by Topham
Picturepoint and the David King Collection

Contents

1 *A* new century

Tsarist Russia

At the beginning of the twentieth century, Russia was ruled by the Romanov royal family. The Tsar (king) was Nicholas II. His coronation in 1894 had been chaotic. Hundreds of people had been trampled to death in a rush for free beer. Some said this was a very bad omen for his reign.

The Tsar was all powerful, but Nicholas himself was not a strong man. Many of his ministers were incompetent and his highly-strung German wife, Alexandra, had considerable influence. Nicholas was a passive man who preferred family life to public affairs.

Historians seeking something good to say about Nicholas sometimes point out that he was a good husband. This he was, but family happiness has never yet saved a dynasty. The lives of Nicholas and Alexandra were tragic because they both had endearing qualities and both found themselves playing roles for which they were quite unfitted. Nicholas … had little choice but to rule.

From *Endurance and Endeavour: Russian History 1812–1992*, by J.N Westwood, 1993

The civil service, the army, and the secret police ran the country for the Tsar. There was no parliament and any opposition to the Government was ruthlessly put down. Nicholas was a very conservative ruler – he was opposed to any change in how Russia was governed. He had absolute power and did not want to give up any of it. But Russia was changing.

At the beginning of the twentieth century, most of Russia's 125 million people lived in the countryside – only 15% lived in towns and cities. Fifty years before, the peasants had been freed from serfdom (a form of slavery). However, by the beginning of the twentieth century, many of them were in serious debt, as they tried to buy their land from their former masters. Many were hungry. Half the peasants had difficulty supporting themselves. There was a famine in Russia in 1891, and another in 1901–1902.

Tsar Nicholas II and Tsarina Alexandra with three of their children

Peasant living conditions at the end of the nineteenth century - basic cottages, and a starving horse pulling a wooden plough

A workers' lodging house in Moscow in 1911. Those workers who were too poor to hire beds, slept on the floor underneath the beds.

C

Russia was beginning to industrialize, however. Foreign investment was bringing new industries, new railways, banks, etc. By 1910, Russia was the fourth largest industrial power in the world. Factories and towns grew up exceptionally quickly with little or no control. As peasants moved to these new towns and mining areas for work, slums grew where conditions were very grim. While the Tsar and his family lived in beautiful palaces where 'an army of servants in gorgeous costumes moved through the polished halls and silken chambers', the conditions of the ordinary people were very different. According to Father Gapon, a Russian Orthodox priest: 'they receive miserable wages and usually live in an overcrowded state, often in special lodging houses. It is common to see ten or more people living in one room, and four sleeping in one bed.' Sometimes men worked 14 or 15 hours a day. Even though trade unions were illegal, strikes were organised to try to improve working conditions. These illegal strikes were brutally put down by the Government.

Nicholas ruled over a vast empire. It stretched from Poland in the west to the Pacific Ocean in the east, and included many different nationalities, for example: 57 million ethnic Russians, 22 million Ukrainians, 6 million Byelorussians, 8 million Poles, 5 million Jews, 3.5 million Tartars, and 1.5 million Germans. Compared with the situation at the beginning of the nineteenth century, the non-Russian population had grown. This was to be a very serious issue for Russian governments throughout the twentieth century.

Conditions for the non-Russian people were difficult. The Tsar's policy was to force all nationalities (Poles, Finns, Tartars, Jews, etc) to become Russian. They were forced to use the Russian language for business and in school. The Russian Orthodox religion became more important than Roman Catholicism or Islam (the other major religions in Russia). However, the Jews, who were numerous in Western Russia, suffered the most. They had to live in certain designated areas. They were also discriminated against in many different ways. Organised attacks (called pogroms) took place on Jewish property and on Jewish homes. This policy of Russification (making everyone Russian) was unpopular and met with resistance. The Russian governor of Finland was assassinated in 1904 in reaction to a policy to Russify Finland.

The different religions practised in Russia were very important. The majority of the population (70%) were Orthodox Christian, 11% were Muslim, and 9% Catholic. Religion was to be a crucial issue for the Communist period because Communism was directly opposed to religion. Russia had its own Church, the Russian Orthodox Church. The Church was very close to the Tsar – he chose the governing body, and the Church supported the Tsar's regime.

The condition of middle class women under Nicholas II was as good in Russia as anywhere else in Europe. By 1908, Russia had female doctors, teachers, and architects. They gained university co-education in 1905. At the same time many young women went abroad to study. Some were exceptional. Sofia Kovalevskaya was unable in the 1880s to enter an all male university in Russia. Like many other ambitious girls, she studied and graduated abroad. Later she became the world's first female professor, as professor of mathematics in Stockholm, Sweden.

Soon after the introduction of co-educational university education, 650 women students enrolled as undergraduates. The women resisted later attempts to put the clock back and exclude them. One woman described how her male student colleagues saw her: 'At first there was embarrassment when we were working on a corpse; the male students regarded us negatively, not having matured sufficiently.'

The conditions for working class and peasant women were much worse. Many had to endure very hard labour in factories and on the farm, and had less food and wages than the men.

Women barge haulers pulling a barge along the River Volga at the end of the nineteenth century

D ▼

Ballet flourished in imperial Russia. The most inventive director was Diaghilev. With dancers like Nijinsky and Pavlova, Russian ballet gained an international reputation. Some of their most inspired work was composed by the most radical composer of the twentieth century – Stravinsky. Russian theatre was equally famous. Chekov's plays were performed across Europe and the acting methods of Stanislavsky are standard practice in the theatre today.

Russia's engineers and scientists led the field in a number of areas – especially strong were hydrodynamics and radio development. They pioneered the use of fuel oil in ships and in trains. Research and development in aviation was also very advanced.

War with Japan

Russia had the longest railway in the world. The Trans-Siberian Railway helped Russia to expand in the east. Here they came into conflict with Japan. Both Russia and Japan wanted to control Manchuria and Korea. The Minister of the Interior, Plehve, encouraged Tsar Nicholas to make war on Japan. He assured him that it would be: 'a merry little war … In order to hold back the revolution we need a small victorious war.' The Japanese had prepared for the war, they had made an alliance with Britain in 1902. Russia, thinking that the Japanese were inferior – Nicholas called them 'little yellow monkeys' – failed to prepare.

The war with Japan (1904–1905) was a disaster for Russia. Japan trounced Russia's army in Manchuria and almost annihilated the Russian Pacific fleet at Port Arthur. Virtually the entire Russian Baltic fleet was then sunk by the Japanese at the Battle of Tsushima in May 1905. Russia was forced to make peace in August 1905 in the Treaty of Portsmouth. Russia had gained nothing. Defeat was humiliating. The war had cost a fortune and showed the government to be corrupt, incompetent, and poorly led. Criticism of the war at home grew as news of the war defeats was received. The war had led to increased prices and food shortages. This added to the general discontent.

Events in the East

1 Decline of China as a power and erosion of Chinese influence in Manchuria and Korea.

2 Japan defeated China in 1895–6. However Russia prevented Japan from taking Port Arthur. Unlike Vladivostok, Port Arthur was ice-free in winter and was of special value to the Russians as a future naval base.

3 Russia created further tension with Japan by occupying Manchuria in 1900 after defeating Chinese forces there.

4 After the defeat of China by Russia, the Russians felt they were superior to any oriental army. Tsar Nicholas called the Japanese 'little monkeys'.

5 However, Japan had become more modern and had developed an efficient army and navy.

6 Britain allied with Japan in 1902. This made it risky for France to help her Russian allies in the event of a Russo-Japanese war.

7 By the end of 1903, Russia had not withdrawn its troops from Manchuria as agreed with Japan. Japan attacked in 1904.

8 After a series of defeats on land and at sea, Russia was forced to make peace with Japan in the Treaty of Portsmouth in August 1905.

▲ The Russo-Japanese War of 1904–1905

▼ A Japanese print of the sinking of the Russian fleet by the Japanese navy in the Russo-Japanese War of 1905

Bloody Sunday

▶ **E**

The initial spark was the dismissal of the four Putilov workmen at the end of December. They were all members of the union. As a mode of pressure Gapon had organised a strike. This enjoyed instant success. By 3rd January all the 13,000 workers were on strike. Within a few days … it was virtually a general strike in the Russian capital.

The authorities were also not idle. By the 7th and 8th January they had assembled troops, including many picked Guards regiments … special concentrations guarded the surroundings of the Winter Palace. The troops set up braziers to warm themselves. It needs little imagination to see St. Petersburg in those January days, as a city on the verge of open conflict.

From *Russia in Revolution,* by L . Kochan, 1970

In January 1905, thousands of unarmed workers marched to the Tsar's Winter Palace in St. Petersburg, led by Father Gapon. Their complaints, which they

wanted to deliver to the Tsar, were numerous: they were concerned about the cost of food; they wanted improved living conditions; and they criticized the war. They also demanded a parliament. Despite all their complaints and hardships, they felt that the Tsar would help them – he was their papa Tsar. In fact, many carried icons of the Tsar on that fateful journey. However, the Tsar was not in his palace. The troops outside fired on the crowd and killed or wounded hundreds of marchers.

Soldiers outside the Winter Palace in St. Petersburg fire on the marchers led by Father Gapon

G

It was an amazing sight. Along came row after row of elderly and solemn workers dressed in their best clothes. Gapon was marching in front carrying a cross and a number of workers were holding icons and portraits of the Tsar. Everyone felt a great sense of excitement. We heard the sound of bugles. The marchers came to a halt, uncertain of what the bugles meant. Just then the cavalry rode out and the first volley was fired in the air, but the second was aimed at the crowd and a number of people fell to the ground. The crowds began running in every direction. They were now being fired on from behind and we took to our heels. The authorities had made a terrible mistake. The workers believed the Tsar would come out to meet them or at least appear on the balcony, but all they got was bullets.

An eyewitness account

Even though the Tsar wasn't there, and, therefore, cannot be blamed for the massacre of innocent people, this attack by his soldiers on unarmed demonstrators began to undermine the Tsar in his people's eyes.

Reaction: reform and repression

Because of the repression in Russia, and the vigilance by the secret police, secret revolutionary groups grew up with the aim of overthrowing the Tsar and his government. After the slaughter on Bloody Sunday 1905, the revolutionary movement gained much strength. Strikes and disorder soon followed. There was mutiny in the army and in the navy. The non-Russian areas, in particular, witnessed very violent disorder. Strikes continued throughout the Summer, culminating in a general strike in

F

We ask but little … reduction of the working day to eight hours, the fixing of wage rates in consultation with us. The construction of factories in which it is possible to work without the risk of death from wind, rain, and snow. Neither we nor the rest of the Russian people enjoy a single human right. We have been enslaved with the help and co-operation of your officials. Anyone who dares to speak up is jailed or exiled. Government by bureaucracy has brought the country to complete ruin, involved in a shameful war and is leading the country further towards disaster. Popular representation is essential.

An extract from the petition that was brought to the Tsar

October which paralysed the country. The revolutionary groups formed a Soviet (a council) in St. Petersburg. This was a type of workers' parliament.

 A poster from 1905 showing the chaos in Russia as a result of Bloody Sunday

The Tsar fearing more chaos, and even a revolution, gave in and issued a manifesto known as the October Manifesto. In it he promised freedom of speech and freedom from unwarranted arrest. He also promised to call a national parliament. For the first time, people could vote. The elections for the first parliament (Duma) were held in 1906. The electorate returned a left wing majority which demanded change. They wanted the land to be given to the peasants, an amnesty for political prisoners, equal rights for all religions, and independence for Poland. They had little co-operation from the Tsar, who refused these demands and closed the Duma.

After a second election which returned another left wing Duma, the Tsar again refused to work with them and dissolved the Duma. He refused to give up much power. He changed the election laws so that he could get the result he wanted. The election of deputies was far less democratic – the upper class were allowed far more deputies; the peasants and the workers far fewer.

While the Tsar was refusing to share power with the Duma, his Prime Minister, Stolypin, ran the country by a policy of repression and reform. He improved the lot of the peasants by ending their payments to free themselves from serfdom. He encouraged them to buy their own land. This allowed a group of fairly rich peasants, kulaks, to emerge. He also introduced some social welfare schemes for workers in the new towns and cities.

However, Stolypin also brutally punished those who opposed the regime. So many were hanged (around 3,000) that the hangman's rope became known as Stolypin's necktie. As a reaction to his repression, he was assassinated in 1911 by a police double agent. Despite his repression, he was far more effective and introduced far more reforms than those ministers who the Tsar appointed after him.

Discontent continued in Russia with frequent strikes – 8,000 from 1912 to 1914. In one strike, which was brutally put down by the secret police and the army, 270 people were killed. Some people thought that the workers were so discontented that the Tsar would not be able to risk mobilising his army for war in 1914.

 Striking workers killed by the authorities at the Lena gold field in Siberia in 1912

1 Describe the condition of the peasants and factory workers, 1900-1914.
2 How difficult was life for Russian women?
3 'Nicholas's decision to go to war with Japan was disasterous.' Do you agree and why?
4 How useful is Source F to historians?
5 Does Source G prove that the demonstration was a serious threat to the Tsar?
6 What do you think people would have thought when they heard about the events of 'Bloody Sunday'?
7 Why did the Tsar refuse to cooperate with the Duma?
8 How do you think Russians would have reacted to the assassination of Stolypin?

Essay: Explain the causes of discontent in Russia, 1900-1914.

2 *T*he fall of the Tsar

Revolutionaries

There was a small group in Russia who wanted fundamental change. They followed the ideas of a German Jew called Karl Marx. He believed that history was the story of the struggle between different classes for power. At that time, the ruling class were the Capitalists; they owned the factories, the banks, etc. According to Marx, they exploited their workers by paying them as little as possible so that they could get as much profit as possible. He believed that the workers would become alienated by this exploitation and rise up against the Capitalists. This revolution, which Marx saw as inevitable, would lead to the workers taking over the means of production (the factories), the means of distribution (the railways), and the methods of exchange (the banks).

The Russian Marxists met in London in 1903 – they were exiled from Russia by the secret police. Their party, the Social Democratic Party, split into two groups. The Mensheviks wanted to take power by becoming a large popular political party, probably working with other Socialist parties to overthrow Capitalism. The Bolsheviks, led by Lenin, wanted a small, tightly-knit, disciplined party, which would seize power on behalf of the industrial workers (the proletariat). A third revolutionary group, called the Social Democrats, wanted the peasants to revolt and take over the land.

Marx believed that a revolution was a scientific inevitability. However, no one expected things to develop so quickly. Lenin said as much in January 1917: 'We of the older generation may not live to see the decisive battles of the coming revolution.'

Russia at war

In August 1914, Germany declared war on Russia. A wave of patriotic fever swept Russia when she joined her allies, Britain and France, in the war against Germany and Austria-Hungary. The capital, St. Petersburg, was renamed Petrograd to make it sound more Russian. Attacks on the Tsar's government became less important than defending the country against Germany.

Russian troops marching to the Central Railway Station in Petrograd on their way to the front

▼

A

The processions in the street carrying the Tsar's portrait, framed in the flag of the allies, the bands everywhere playing the National Anthem.

… the long unending line of khaki-clad figures who marched away singing and cheering, tall bronzed men with honest open faces with childlike eyes and a trusting faith in the little father (Nicholas II), and a sure and certain hope that the saints would protect them and bring them back to their villages …

Those first days of war! How full we were of enthusiasm, of the conviction that we were fighting in a just and holy cause, for the freedom and betterment of the world! Swept away by the general air of excitement, we dreamt dreams of triumph and victory! The Russian steamroller! The British navy! The French guns! The war would be over by Christmas. The Cossacks would ride into Berlin.

From Muriel Buchanan (daughter of the British Ambassador to Russia) writing in 1914, when Germany declared war on Russia

As Muriel Buchanan says, they expected the war to be over in a few months. Instead it dragged on for years. She also illustrates what Russia's contribution to the allied effort was to be – a human steamroller, made up of millions of men. Fifteen million men were mobilised, but they were scandalously badly supplied. It is estimated that up to a quarter of the troops went to the front without weapons. Imagine men being sent into battle without a gun, having to wait until a comrade dropped before they could defend themselves. Few of the men had decent boots or enough bowls and cups to eat and drink from!

B ▼

> General Rudski had complained to me of the lack of ammunition and the poor equipment for the men. There was a lack of ammunition and a great shortage of boots. In the Carpathians the soldiers fought barefooted. The Grand Duke (Commander-in-Chief) stated that he was obliged to stop fighting temporarily for lack of ammunition and boots.

From the Memoirs of Rodzianko, President of the Duma, writing about the war situation in the winter of 1915

The war went very badly. Russia suffered more defeats and more casualties than any other country in the war. With the war going badly, the Tsar's response was to sack his Commander-in-Chief and appoint himself in charge of the war effort. This was brave but foolish. He would now be held directly responsible for all the disasters in the war.

German troops guarding Russian boy soldiers captured after the Battle of Tannenberg, 1915

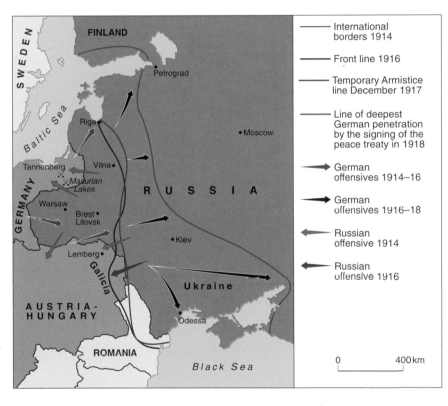
The Eastern Front in the First World War

Russian soldiers kneel before the Tsar as he blesses them before battle

Rasputin

While the Tsar was at the front, his wife was left in charge of the Government. She was even less politically competent than he was. She was also deeply unpopular – to many she was 'that German woman'. Increasingly, she came under the hypnotic influence of Rasputin, a peasant monk who could control the bleeding of her haemophiliac son Alexi. Alexi used to bleed uncontrollably, but mysteriously under Rasputin's influence the bleeding would stop – possibly he calmed him hypnotically. Whatever the explanation, to her he was a holy man who saved her son from certain death. To others he was a corrupt, drunken womaniser who had too much influence.

The Tsarina was too reliant on his advice. He persuaded her to change government ministers and appoint others of his choosing who were weak, incompetent, and unpopular. In two years there were four Prime Ministers and four Ministers of War – while the country was trying to wage a war!

I am haunted by our friend's (Rasputin's) wish, and know it will be fatal for us and the country if it is not fulfilled.
I have absolutely no faith in Grand Duke Nicholas. You know Nicholas' hatred of Gregory (Rasputin) is intense. Russia will not be blessed if her sovereign lets a man of God be persecuted.

The Tsarina writing in 1915 to the Tsar, advising him to replace Grand Duke Nicholas as Commander-in-Chief.

This Russian cartoon shows Rasputin's influence over the Tsar and Tsarina

E

I must give you a message from our friend Rasputin prompted by what he saw in the night. He begs you to order an advance near Riga ... otherwise the Germans will settle down through all the winter ... he says we can and we must and I was to write to you at once.

Extracts from a letter by the Tsarina to the Tsar, 28th November 1915

Rasputin surrounded by his court followers

In 1916, a group of noblemen who recognised Rasputin's destructive influence murdered him. Even his death seemed bizarre – he was poisoned, shot, beaten, and then drowned!

However, Rasputin's death could not solve the problems of the country. The Russian economy could not meet the needs of both the soldiers at the front and the people at home. The railway system was unable to deliver military supplies to the front or food to the cities. With 15 million men (mostly peasants) in the army, not enough food was produced on the farms. There was widespread hunger, especially in 1917. As the people were also short of coal, they were both cold and hungry.

I aimed at his heart and pulled the trigger ... Rasputin lay on his back. Our hearts were full of hope for we were convinced that what had just taken place would save Russia and the Dynasty from ruin. and dishonour.

... Then a terrible thing happened: with a sudden violent effort Rasputin leapt to his feet foaming at the mouth.

... Two shots echoed through the night ... I saw Rasputin totter and fall beside a heap of snow.

From *Lost Splendour,* by Prince Yusopov, 1953

February Revolution

There were strikes and demonstrations in reaction to the shortages. The largest of these was at the giant Putilov works where 30,000 men were employed. There was no coal to run the works. On international women's day, 23rd February 1917, a group of women marched through Petrograd. They were fed up with the endless queues for food.

Moscow, 1917 – the sign in the shop window reads 'no bread will be distributed today'

Soon 90,000 more joined them calling for bread. According to the police reports: 'The workers had gone on strike in protest against the shortage of black bread. As the strike spread all the factories stopped working. Other workmen walked in crowds into the streets shouting "Give us bread" ... order was restored only towards 7.00 pm'.

Within three days 250,000 were on strike. The Tsar ordered the army to put down the revolt but the army mutinied, refused to fire on the crowd, and joined the strikers.

... the tips of the bayonets were touching the breasts of the front row of demonstrators. Behind could be heard the singing of revolutionary songs, in front there was confusion. Women with tears in their eyes were crying out to the soldiers 'Comrades, take away your bayonets, join us!' The soldiers were moved. They threw quick glances at their own comrades. The next moment one bayonet is slowly raised, is slowly lifted above the shoulders of the approaching demonstrators. There is thunderous applause. The triumphant crowd greeted their brothers clothed in the grey cloaks of the soldiery. The soldiers mixed freely with the demonstrators.

A Bolshevik eyewitness describes how the soldiers joined the strikers

The people of Petrograd turned to the Duma, which up until now had been loyal to the Tsar, for leadership. The Duma organised a provisional (temporary) government. They wanted to end autocracy (rule by one man) and set up a parliamentary government. The Tsar tried to get back to Petrograd, but his train was stopped by soldiers. He had lost all political support and he was persuaded by his generals and leading politicians to abdicate (give up the throne).

H

> The Tsar received a telegram from the Chief of Staff stating bluntly that the war could be continued only if the Tsar abdicated in favour of his son.
>
> Every moment lost would lead to further demands by the revolutionists who now controlled the railroads and supply service for the army ... Later all the generals agreed with this: 'But how do I know that it is the desire of all Russia?'. 'Your majesty' replied one 'circumstances prevent us sending out questionnaires on this matter.'
>
> ' ...I have made up my mind, I am abdicating ...' He made the sign of the cross.

From *Lenin,* by David Shub, 1965

The Romanov dynasty had come to an end.

Provisional Government

The new Provisional Government faced a difficult task. They took over a country in chaos. The war was going badly, and the food shortages and economic crisis had led to a revolutionary mood in the country. In the countryside, the peasants burned and looted the landlords' houses, and demanded their own land. Soldiers and workers set up soviets to run the factories and the towns. The workers wanted food; the national minorities independence; and the soldiers wanted an end to the war.

At the same time another powerful group was formed. The soldiers and workers formed a workers' government in Petrograd, the Petrograd Soviet. The Petrograd Soviet accepted the Provisional Government as the legitimate government; and did not try to take power because they believed that their time had not yet come. However, the Provisional Government could not govern without them. The Soviet, in Order Number One, called on the soldiers to elect representatives to command their units, except in battle – clearly a revolutionary exhortation. The soldiers were only to obey the Provisional Government if the Soviet agreed with the orders – a recipe for disaster.

The Provisional Government promised reform. They knew that they had to tackle the problem of land reform and they intended to, but not immediately. Naturally, the peasants, to whom owning their own land was all important, were bitterly disappointed with the Provisional Government. The national minorities (Poles, Finns, Tartars, etc) hoped that the new regime would mean more autonomy, even independence, for them. But they too were to be disappointed. The Provisional Government asked the minorities to wait.

The worst decision of the Government was to continue with the war. They felt that they had to honour their commitments to their allies and keep Russia in the war. Keeping Germany fighting on two fronts – against Russia in the east and Britain and

This famous photograph shows a loyal Russian soldier trying to stop two comrades deserting

▼

France in the west – helped to win the war for the allies. However, Russia continued to suffer humiliating defeats. Discipline and morale in the army broke down, and desertion was commonplace.

To add to Prime Minister Kerensky's troubles, the Germans sent revolutionaries back to Russia, expecting them to stir up trouble and revolution. Lenin, the leader of the Bolsheviks, arrived in Petrograd in April. His message was simple and popular: 'Peace, Bread, and Land'. He knew that the country was tired of war, hungry for food, and that the peasants wanted to own land. This slogan was much more popular than the Government's policy of pursuing the war. Lenin refused to co-operate with the Provisional Government. He claimed that the real revolution was yet to come, with the workers and the peasants taking power. The Provisional Government's liberal policies were not enough for Lenin. They had introduced some very liberal measures in a country that had only known autocracy. They had granted: free speech; political amnesty (freedom) to all political prisoners; equality for all, i.e all religions, all classes, and all nationalities; and a parliament elected by all. However, Lenin wanted more fundamental change than this. He wanted the peasants and the workers to own the means of production, the means of distribution, and the methods of exchange. Even though the Tsar had been overthrown; liberal policies were being introduced; and the war was still going on; Lenin called for a second revolution to overthrow the Provisional Government and set up a Communist regime in Russia.

Demonstrators gathered outside the Duma in Petrograd in 1917. Their banners read 'Land and Freedom'.

1 Briefly explain 'Marxism'.
2 Why was St Petersburg renamed Petrograd?
3 How useful is Source A?
4 How do you think the soldiers would have felt about the situation described in Source B?
5 How do Sources C and E support the opinion of the cartoonist in Source D?
6 How reliable is Source H about the events of the Tsar's abdication?
7 How did Russia's involvement in the First World War lead to the end of the Tsar's rule?
8 Was the Provisional Government bound to fail?

Essay: Was Nicholas II responsible for his own downfall?

3 *The* Bolsheviks take power

The war goes badly

Lenin's return to Petrograd in April 1917 changed everything. He called for a second revolution to overthrow the Provisional Government and give power to the workers and the peasants. Kerensky and the Provisional Government had decided to continue the war. Lenin, on the other hand, opposed the war and demanded peace.

In June, the Provisional Government launched an attack on the Germans. Russia was badly defeated. The continuing defeats led to demonstrations against the war. The demands for peace grew. At the same time, rebellion seethed among the national minorities who wanted more autonomy and were disappointed by the unwillingness of the Provisional Government to grant them their independence. By July, the soldiers in Petrograd were so fed up with the food shortages that they attacked Government buildings. The Bolsheviks supported the uprising, but the attempt was premature. Troops loyal to the Government put down the rebellion in two days. The July Days showed that the time wasn't ripe – yet – for a revolution. The Provisional Government claimed that the Bolsheviks were German agents and arrested and imprisoned the leaders. Lenin escaped to Finland.

Troops loyal to the Provisional Government fire on Bolshevik rebels at Petrograd in July 1917

Peasants and army deserters looting and burning a noble's country house in 1917

Despite this victory, the Government was losing control. The peasants were simply taking the land for themselves. Thousands of soldiers deserted, returning to their villages to join in the land grab. The Bolshevik message of 'Peace, Bread, and Land' was much more popular than the Government's decision to continue the war, and their reluctance to reform the land system. When Lenin returned in April, the Bolsheviks were not in a majority on the Soviets. The decision to continue the war gave it to them. By September, they had control of the Petrograd and Moscow Soviets – the most important two.

In September, General Kornilov, who had recently been appointed Commander-in-Chief of the army, began to move his troops towards Petrograd, possibly initially in response to a request from Kerensky to restore order and put down the Soviet. As Kornilov approached Petrograd, Kerensky suddenly accused him of attempting a coup d'état (taking over the Government by force). Kerensky armed the workers in order to defend the capital. The Bolshevik leaders were released from prison and given weapons. The railwaymen went on strike and prevented Kornilov from entering the city. The city was saved, the coup failed, but the Kornilov affair was an embarrassment for Kerensky. The Bolsheviks grew in popularity and were now rearmed.

The October Revolution

Throughout September and October, Lenin constantly wrote to the other Bolshevik leaders urging them to take power. He returned to Petrograd from Finland in disguise, and began to persuade the others on the Central Committee that the time was ripe for an armed insurrection. He argued that: 'History will not forgive us if we do not take power now'.

The Bolsheviks were supported by the soldiers in the Petrograd garrison and the sailors at Kronstadt naval base. On 24th October, the Red Guards, on Trotsky's orders, took over the key points in Petrograd (the telephone exchange, railway stations etc). The cruiser *Aurora* sailed up the River Neva and shelled the Provisional Government in the Winter Palace. The coup itself was a bloodless affair. The Red Guards (the Bolshevik soldiers) simply arrested the Provisional Government as they sat around the cabinet table discussing the crisis. A young Bolshevik announced: 'In the name of the Military and the Revolutionary Committee of the Petrograd Soviet, I declare the Provisional Government deposed.' Kerensky escaped in an American Embassy car. He tried to rally troops to the cause of the Provisional Government but without much success.

The Congress of Soviets was meeting in the Smolny Institute – previously a school for young ladies. Lenin addressed them: 'We shall now proceed to construct the Socialist order.'

Accounts of the events leading up to the October Revolution and the Revolution itself vary considerably. The most popular visual images of the October Revolution come from a film called 'October', made in 1927 by Sergei Eisenstein, a Soviet film maker.

A

On the 10th of October Lenin showed at the Central Committee that the moment was ripe for the seizure of power by the proletariat and the poor peasants. The Central Committee adopted Lenin's historic resolution on the armed uprising. Kamenev and Zinoviev alone acted as cowards and opposed the resolution ... the uprising was carried out with true military precision and still in full accord with Lenin's instructions. The fighting units acted with a high degree of organisation, discipline and co-ordination.

In his guidance of the uprising, Lenin's genius as a leader of the masses, a wise and fearless strategist, who clearly saw what direction the revolution would take, was strikingly revealed.

From *V.I Lenin – A Short Biography,* by G.D. Obichkin, 1976. This is an official Soviet biography of Lenin

B

For many years, particularly in the Stalin period, the evidence of Lenin's violent controversy with his colleagues over the uprising was concealed in Party archives. Even today the facts are not all known. And even after Lenin's victory on October 10th there was another big argument on the 15th. Lenin had the firm support of 15 out of the 25 members present; but an important faction of the party, centred around two of the most prominent members, Kamenev and Zinoviev, felt that the uprising would be a disaster. Kerensky did not bother to order additional troops into the capital. Bolshevik plans went forward lackadaisically ... anger and energy spent, Lenin now seemed to sink into a kind of lethargy. So far as the record goes he did little or nothing from the 20th to the 23rd of October.

From *Russia in Revolution,* by Harrison E. Salisbury, 1978. The author was Moscow correspondent to *The New York Times.*

D

Cameras at that time couldn't shoot in darkness, so there are no contemporary newsreels or photographs of the Revolution. In fact there was no mass storming of the Winter Palace; it was much less dramatic and more disorganised. The American journalist John Reed (a Communist sympathiser) gave this account by a sailor who took part in the assault on the Winter Palace:

'About 11 o'clock we broke in the doors and we filtered up different stairways one by one, or in little bunches. When we got to the top of the stairs the officer cadets took away our guns; still our fellows kept coming up, little by little until we had a majority. Then we turned around and we took away the cadets' guns.'

Eisenstein used live ammunition when making the film 'October'. More people were injured and more damage done to the Palace in making the film than during the Revolution itself.

From *Timewatch,* a BBC history investigation programme, 1987

C

This still from Eisenstein's film 'October', shows Lenin standing on an armoured car at the Winter Palace, urging the Red Guards forward

E

This picture by P. Sokolov-Skalya gives another interpretation of the storming of the Winter Palace

The Bolsheviks in power

A week after they took power, the long promised elections to the Constituent Assembly (Parliament) were held. The Bolsheviks only polled 9 million votes compared with 21 million for the Social Revolutionaries. Even though the Bolsheviks only won a quarter of the seats, they had no intention of handing over power. Lenin argued that the Social Revolutionaries – who had won the election – were the party of the past because they represented the peasants. As the future belonged to the industrial classes (the proletariat), who he represented, then he should keep power on their behalf. Red Guards evacuated the delegates and barred the doors of the Parliament. There were to be no more free elections. The Bolsheviks renamed their party the Communist Party in 1918.

The Bolsheviks began to rule by decree or declarations. Ownership of land was to be in the hands of the State. The Tsar's land, the Church's land, and the nobles' land was to be given to the local Soviet. The peasants had not expected the State to take over the land on their behalf. They simply ignored the Soviets' claims to ownership and divided the land among themselves.

The workers were given control over running the factories. Just as the peasants were free from their landlords and the workers free from the Capitalists, all Russian people were declared to be free and equal. However, people were not free to believe or to think independently. Religion was banned, and newspapers that did not support the Bolshevik regime were shut down.

Another decree gave the national minorities the right to leave Russia and form autonomous states. Lenin was well aware that Russia was multinational. He wanted the non-Russian people to be attracted to Communism – he wanted to persuade them of the advantages of belonging to one Communist country. His policy was to allow all nationalities to be free to join the new Communist state or to become independent. Lenin believed that if the nationalities did not feel repressed, they would forget their nationality and realise they were the working class whose common interests were best served by Socialism. Accordingly, the Declaration of the Rights of the Peoples of Russia was issued on 5th November 1917. It said: 'Any nation has the right to set up its own state'. The Soviet state was to be a federal state.

However, Lenin and the Bolsheviks were surprised when a number of the nationalities actually wanted to break away – the Poles, Finns, and Ukrainians all wanted independence. The Bolshevik policy of freedom of choice was abandoned. Instead they decided to re-establish control. Gradually they reasserted control over the Ukraine, Azerbaijan, Armenia, and

Georgia. The Union was held together by military force and victory in the Civil War. Stalin, the Commissar for Nationalities, said that it was not in the interests of the people to leave the Union, which would lead to victory for the counter-Revolution. However, a number of independent states were formed, such as Poland, Finland, Estonia, and Latvia. At the Party Congress in 1922, a new name was adopted to reflect the new federal state – the Union of Soviet Socialist Republics (USSR).

The Jews had been victims in Tsarist Russia of organised racist attacks (pogroms). Thousands of Jews were also massacred in the Civil War by the White armies. Initially the Communists banned anti-Semitism. However, when Trotsky, who was himself Jewish, lost influence, anti-Semitism returned. Like the other believers, Jews were barred from freely practising their religion.

An anti-Semitic, anti-Trotsky poster published by the Whites in the Civil War. Trotsky, as well as being Jewish, was in charge of the Red Army during the Civil War.

The situation after 1917 was extraordinary. A very small atheistic group were now ruling a largely religious country. Lenin despised religion because, like Marx, he believed it was the opium of the masses, taking their minds off the necessity for revolution against the bosses. Realizing that the religious beliefs and conviction of the people were too deep to overthrow, he decided instead to attack the Church as an organisation. Severe anti-religious legislation was passed – priests could only meet with official permission; Sunday schools were closed; and the religious instruction of children became a crime. The State took away the land from the Church. They closed down countless monasteries which were turned into hospitals or army barracks. The Russian Orthodox Church lost all its legal rights. Many priests and monks were badly treated – some imprisoned, others executed. The State began to undermine religion in every possible way – by propaganda and by making it very difficult for people to pray and to worship. Religion was mocked by the new government.

G Anti-religious graffiti painted on the wall of a Moscow monastery. It is accusing the priests and monks of taking money from the starving peasants to pay for their own debauched lifestyle.

Solzhenitsyn says that the destruction of religion was one of the main aims of the Communists: 'Monks and nuns whose black habits had been a distinctive feature of old Russian life were intensively rounded up, placed under arrest and sent into exile … the circles kept getting bigger as they raked in ordinary believers as well, old people and particularly women who were the most stubborn believers of all'.

The leaders of the Russian Orthodox Church tried to work with the Communist authorities by recognising the new atheistic state, openly declaring their loyalty, even when their churches were being closed, and priests and nuns were being put into jail. By 1920, 330 priests and bishops had been executed. Many who were executed had defiantly opposed the new regime. The Church leaders believed that swallowing their pride and compromising with the new State would allow the Church to continue in the Soviet Union.

Women and the Revolution

Women played an active part on both sides in the Revolutions of 1917 and the subsequent Civil War.

The February Revolution, which had led to the abdication of the Tsar, began when the women of Petrograd took to the streets demanding bread because their children were starving. They implored the soldiers who had been sent to put down the strike to join them. The soldiers did. However, there were also women in the Tsar's army, and some saw active service. The new Provisional Government was guarded in the Winter Palace by the Women's Death Battalion. Once the Red Army was formed, many women decided to join it. A significant number of women also worked in the CHEKA or secret police, gathering intelligence and spying. It has been estimated that as many as 70,000 women fought in the Civil War.

Soldiers of the Women's Death Battalion guarding the Provisional Government in the Winter Palace in 1917

▼

After the Bolshevik take-over, women gained positions of influence in the Communist Party. Elena Stasova rose to become General Secretary of the Party, while Angelica Balabanova became Ukrainian Foreign Minister and Secretary of the Comintern. The most important female figure in the Revolution was Aleksendra Kollantai, who was a member of the Central Committee and Commissar of Public Welfare, and later Ambassador to Sweden. The Bolshevik Revolution proclaimed the equality of the sexes. However, only four women made it to the influential Central Committee.

Those outside the Communist Party believed that the Bolshevik policies would break up families. Many men fought what they saw as the Bolshevik attempt to make their wives political. One significant change was the replacing of Church weddings with civil marriage. Divorce was also made simple and the numbers of common law marriages grew, as did the numbers of deserted wives.

Lenin felt that the Soviet government had done more than any other country to emancipate women. Kollantai saw things differently: 'The Revolution has brought rights on paper but in fact it has made life much harder for women'. Many women were exhausted by the double workload of factory and home (few men helped at home). Many families were also left without a father after the First World War and the Civil War. The orphan problem reached huge proportions, with thousands of children simply roaming the streets. Food was in short supply and famine stalked the land during the Civil War.

Peace with Germany

Lenin had promised peace and he wanted peace at any price. Trotsky, in charge of the Bolshevik forces, wanted to delay by negotiating with the Germans. Trotsky wanted to negotiate a settlement where they stopped fighting, but didn't end the War. This proposal of 'neither peace nor war' was unacceptable to the Germans.

This would have brought the fighting to an end, but their troops would still have been tied down on the Eastern Front. They wanted them released for a final push on the Western Front. Disregarding this negotiating tactic of Trotsky's, the Germans pressed on with the war. By now the Russian army was a shambles. Germany captured large areas of Russian land. Russia was finally forced to make peace at the Treaty of Brest-Litovsk in March 1918. The Germans extracted a heavy price – Russia lost about one third of her population, one third of her agricultural land, and about two thirds of her heavy industry. But at least the war was over. Bolshevik Russia had other enemies to worry about.

Russian territory lost in the Treaty of Brest-Litovsk, March 1918

Map legend:
- Russian frontier in 1914
- Russian frontier after the Treaty of Brest Litovsk
- Russian lands lost at the Treaty of Brest Litovsk
- 0 — 400km

The Civil War, 1918–1921

Western countries like Britain and France were critical of Russia leaving the war, which broke earlier treaties and allowed the Germans to fight the war on one front. They also feared Communism and they knew that the Bolsheviks intended to export their revolution to every other country. The senior Russian army officers hated the humiliating terms of the Treaty of Brest-Litovsk and wanted to regain control of the army. Understandably, the landowners were opposed to the land decrees which at a stroke had taken their land, power, and influence away from them. Even the other Socialists, like the Social Revolutionaries who had won the election and were denied power by the Bolsheviks, were vehemently opposed to them. The national minorities were also anxious to break away from this new state and set up independent states in their own areas. All of these forces of opposition to the Bolsheviks joined together in a very loose alliance in a Civil War against the Bolsheviks.

To defend the Revolution against attack, Lenin and Trotsky set up the Red Army and the CHEKA (the secret police). After an unsuccessful attempt on Lenin's life and the assassination of the CHEKA boss, the CHEKA took a terrible revenge. They killed numerous enemies in an affair known as the Red Terror.

Trotsky was in charge of the Red Army throughout the Civil War. Extensive and effective use was made of propaganda posters to whip up enthusiasm for the war. Within three years the Red Army had grown to five million men. Throughout the war, both sides used cruelty and terror as weapons. Both sides were guilty of pogroms against the Jews.

The Tsar and his family had remained as prisoners after his abdication. They were kept at Ekaterinburg in the Ural Mountains. He was the one figure around whom the opponents to the new regime could have united – for they were a disunited opposition. However, in July 1918 local Bolsheviks, probably without Lenin's knowledge, shot the Tsar, his wife, and their children.

I A Bolshevik Civil War poster from 1919. It shows the three main White commanders, General Denikin, Admiral Kolchak, and General Yudenich, being controlled by the main interventionist powers, Britain, France, and the USA.

J 'Shoulder to shoulder in the defence of Petrograd'. This poster was published by the Bolsheviks in 1919 when Petrograd was threatened by General Yudenich's White forces.

When the Civil War broke out, the Red Army was hemmed in around Moscow and Petrograd. Within three years they had expelled the interventionist and counter-

Revolutionary forces and pushed the Polish army back to Warsaw. How did they do it against so much opposition?

1 They were more popular than the Whites.

2 The Whites were disunited and with no single leader. Each of the White generals had his own army, which did not support or reinforce the work of the others. They were only united in their opposition to the Bolsheviks. Socialists, royalists, and army generals were unlikely to have common policies on how to run the country after the war.

3 Trotsky ruled the Red Army with a rod of iron. Unauthorised retreat was punishable by death.

4 The Red Army controlled the railways, which ensured supplies and troops could be sent quickly anywhere. They also controlled the main cities of Moscow and Petrograd with their factories.

▶ Trotsky lecturing soldiers of the newly-formed Red Army in 1918

The Civil War, 1918–1921
▼

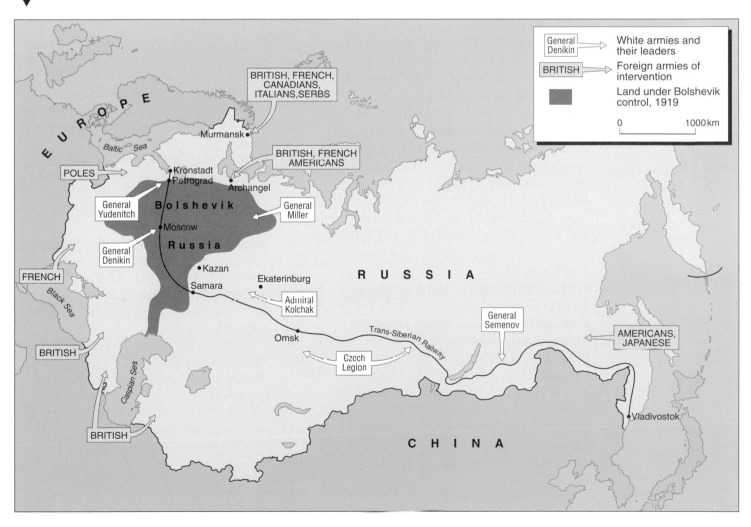

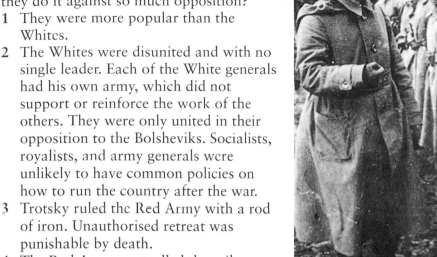

Lenin had to ensure that the army were fed and well supplied. He did this by a policy known as War Communism. The Government took over all the important industries, and food had to be supplied to the Government at a fixed rate which was very low. The State gave itself the power – and it used it – to seize grain from any reluctant peasants to feed the factory workers and the soldiers. Nobody was allowed to sell any goods for their own profit. Workers in the factories had to follow Government orders to supply fixed quotas of goods. Failure to comply brought the death penalty.

The result of this War Communism was chaos. Peasants refused to hand over the food, or failed to plant crops that they knew would be taken. Many people did not receive enough rations to live on. The situation in the factories was just as chaotic with managers fleeing abroad and workers refusing to work for starvation wages.

By 1921, famine had broken out. Industrial production was down to one seventh of the 1913 level. It is estimated that 3.5 million people died from typhoid alone. With the economy in ruins; inflation out of control; and the country in the grip of famine; the peasants called for the overthrow of Communism. They rose up against the army and the CHEKA. Lenin was so concerned that he said: 'we are barely hanging on'. Again the Bolsheviks responded with terror. They imposed their will by rounding up villagers and shooting them in batches; whole villages were also sent into exile.

However, they had to face a more serious revolt when, in 1921, the sailors at Kronstadt mutinied, demanding more political and economic freedom. They had always been regarded as the most loyal supporters of the Bolsheviks. Although Trotsky and the Red Army put down the revolt, the Party realised that if even their most loyal supporters were revolting against them, then it was time to change the policies that were driving them into revolt.

War Communism was replaced by the New Economic Policy, which allowed free trade and profit. Peasants were now expected to pay a fixed tax in grain and other food. If they grew more food than this, they were allowed to sell it at a profit. The increased production helped to reduce the threat of famine. Private enterprise was also allowed to return to industry. By 1924 the State still owned and ran 98% of large scale industry, but 80% of the smaller factories were privately run. A new rouble (the unit of currency) was introduced in 1922 to help to stabilize the economy; and foreign trade and investment were encouraged.

By 1926, in most areas, the economy had regained the 1913 level of output. However, this meant that Russian industry was still very backward compared with other countries. The NEP had also meant the relaxation of a number of Socialist principles, such as State ownership of the means of production – the factories.

1   How do Sources A and B differ in their accounts of Lenin's role in the Revolution?
2   i) How reliable are Sources A and B?
    ii) What other information would be helpful?
3   i) How much support did the Bolsheviks have?
    ii) Were they entitled to seize power?
4   Was the position of women better or worse after the Revolution?
5   Under the Bolsheviks did people have more or less freedom?
6   What was the significance of changing the country's name to the USSR?
7   Why did Russia give up so much territory to Germany in the Treaty of Brest-Litovsk?
8   Describe the Bolshevik attitude towards religion.
9   i) What was the purpose of the posters, Sources I and J?
    ii) How effectively did they achieve their objectives?
10 Why did the Bolsheviks win the Civil War?
11 Why did Lenin replace War Communism with the New Economic Policy?

Essay: Describe the events in Russia from the October Revolution until 1922.

4. Stalin takes control

Heirs to the throne

Lenin was the undisputed leader of Communist Russia. During the Revolution and the Civil War, he forced the rest of the leadership to go along with him. But his health was failing from 1922 onwards. Who would succeed him as leader? How would a new leader be chosen? In a monarchy the monarch's eldest son takes over, and in a democracy the people vote for a new leader. But Communist Russia had no organised system ready to select a new leader in the event of Lenin's death.

Before his death in 1924, Lenin wrote about all the other senior figures in the Party. He outlined their strengths and weaknesses. Two leaders stood out among these as the most important and, in the event of Lenin's death, the most likely to succeed him. They were Trotsky and Stalin.

A

Comrade Stalin, having become General Secretary, has too much power in his hands; and I am not sure that he always knows how to use that power with sufficient caution ... Stalin is too coarse and this fault is unsupportable in the office of General Secretary. Therefore I propose to the comrades to remove Stalin from the position and appoint to it another man who will in all respects differ from Stalin – more patient, more loyal, more polite, more attentive to comrades. Trotsky is the most able man in the Party. His defect is an excess of self-confidence. He is attracted too much by the purely administrative aspect of affairs.

From Lenin's last will and testament

Lenin felt that no single ruler should take his place.

Trotsky, according to Lenin, was the most capable but was too self assured. Stalin, he felt, had concentrated too much power in his hands and he was unsure if he would use that power cautiously. Stalin had been very rude to Lenin's wife and Lenin recommended that Stalin be removed from his post. Lenin was specifically concerned with the way that Stalin as Commissar for Nationalities was treating the national minorities. Even though Stalin was a Georgian himself, he was ruthlessly opposed to any independence for the nationalities. Because of his treatment of them, all the Bolshevik Central Committee in Georgia resigned. Lenin set up an investigation and discovered that they resigned because of Stalin's bullying.

Trotsky seemed to many to be the natural successor to Lenin. He was brilliant both as a writer and as a leader. He had led the Red Army in the Civil War with great success. He had also planned much of the 1917 October Revolution. But he wasn't well liked. Some resented the fact that he was an ex-Menshevik who joined the Party late – just before the Revolution in fact. But the real fear was that he would take power with the help of the army (the Russian Revolution would resemble the French when Napoleon became the military leader after the Revolution). Stalin had joined forces with Zinoviev and Kamenev to keep Trotsky out. These three (the Troika) emphasized Trotsky's disagreements with Lenin to discredit him. When Lenin called for Stalin's removal, Kamenev and Zinoviev supported Stalin. They said that Lenin was mistaken in his views on Stalin. They had helped Stalin to survive.

There was only one chance for the Communist Party to get rid of Stalin, and that was in May 1924 when Lenin's will was read out to the Central Committee. One eyewitness later wrote: 'Stalin sitting on the steps of the rostrum looked small and miserable; in spite of his self control and show of calm it was clearly evident that his fate was at stake'. Zinoviev was very anxious not to lose Stalin's help in the struggle against Trotsky and so smoothly and smilingly he suggested that the will not be published, for Comrade Lenin's suspicions of Stalin had been proved baseless. The others agreed, especially as the will contained criticisms of them too. Lenin's widow jumped to her feet to protest at this suppression of her husband's will, but in vain. Stalin sat quietly wiping the sweat from his brow.

From *Stalin: man of steel,* by Elizabeth Roberts, 1968

Lenin had a stroke in 1922, probably as a result of overwork. He never fully recovered to play the active dominant part he had before. He died in January 1924 from a brain haemorrhage. Much to his widow's annoyance, Stalin developed a semi-religious cult around the dead Lenin. An immortalisation committee was set up to ensure his cult status; a huge mausoleum was built to display his body; Petrograd was renamed Leningrad; some even wanted Sunday to be renamed Lenin day. Stalin exploited this cult to his own advantage. He was the chief mourner at Lenin's funeral. Trotsky was not at the funeral.

A photograph, published after Lenin's death in 1924, showing Stalin as the chief mourner at his funeral

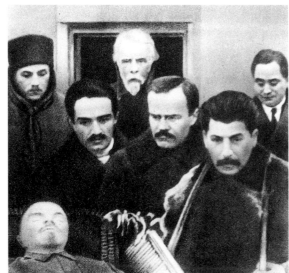

Trotsky was recovering from an illness when Lenin died. He telephoned Stalin to ask when the funeral was to be. Stalin said: 'On Saturday, you can't get back in time anyway so we advise you to continue with your treatment'. This was a lie, the funeral was not to be until Sunday and Trotsky could have reached Moscow by then.

From *Leon Trotsky, The Eternal Rebel,* by Ronald Seth, 1967

The person who was seen to be closest to Lenin was likely to inherit his authority. Each of the contenders tried to emphasize how close they were to him. Trotsky and Zinoviev tried to show they were colleagues of Lenin, his equal. Stalin adopted the more humble pose of Lenin's disciple. Photos were used to show that he was a devoted pupil of Lenin's. His presentation of Lenin's doctrines in a simple way was very popular and effective.

Photographs like this were used by Stalin to demonstrate that he was Lenin's disciple

The rise of Stalin

Stalin held a number of important posts: Commissar of Nationalities, member of the Politburo and Orgburo. But his great power base was in the Party. He was the Party Secretary. The other, more intellectual and flamboyant leaders thought that as Stalin was dull (he was called a grey blur, a mediocrity) he was suited to the monotonous administrative work of Party Secretary. However, he was able to appoint his own supporters to positions of influence in the Party. Those he appointed and promoted felt grateful to him and supported him. The Party grew rapidly from 700,000 to 1,700,000. Many of the new recruits to the Party were less well educated than the earlier members and they liked Stalin's simplified interpretation of Marxism.

The great debate in the Party was about how to secure Communism. Trotsky advocated spreading the revolution around the world. The fledgling Communist state in Russia could only be guaranteed if Communism was established elsewhere. Stalin disagreed. He argued that Socialism in Russia could be secured without the aid of other countries. This policy of 'Socialism in one country' suggested that he had confidence in the workers and peasants in Russia. This appealed to a nationalist sense of pride. When Communist revolts had failed elsewhere, e.g. in Germany, Stalin's policy seemed more attractive.

The decline of Trotsky

The threat from Trotsky eased and he was removed from his post as Commissar of War in January 1925.

Trotsky's power was in the formidable Red Army of which he was the supreme commander. There was little doubt that it would support him if he tried to seize power. Stalin therefore proposed to the Central Committee of the Party that Comrade Trotsky be removed from his position as head of the army for the war had been over for some time and it was a pity to waste his brilliant talents. Comrade Trotsky should be put in charge of the electrification of the USSR. The Committee duly elected Trotsky to this new post.

From *Stalin: man of steel,* by Elizabeth Roberts, 1968

Trotsky had now lost his most effective weapon. He asked himself how he had lost power (Source F):

'How could I have lost power? A division began to reveal itself between the leaders ... If I took no part in these amusements ... it was because I hated to inflict such boredom on myself. The new ruling group felt that I didn't fit in; many group conversations would stop the moment I appeared. This was a definite indication that I had begun to lose power.'

Trotsky during the years of argument, sometimes sat silent in the Central Committee, he was once seen reading a novel ... Trotsky was ill during the the winters of 1924 and 1925 and went on a cure to Berlin in 1926. He wrote: 'My high temperature paralyses me at the most critical moments and acts as my opponents' most steadfast ally ...'

He and his supporters in congresses and committees were increasingly heckled and shouted down; outside they found their meetings broken up by thugs.

From *The Assassination of Trotsky,* by Nicholas Mosley, 1972

With the threat from Trotsky receding, Stalin no longer needed his old allies Zinoviev and Kamenev. Zinoviev disagreed with Stalin at the 9th Party Congress. But as the Congress was packed with men loyal to Stalin, Zinoviev was easily defeated. Soon Zinoviev was to lose his post as boss of Leningrad. By 1926 neither Zinoviev nor Kamenev had much power left. In 1927 Trotsky and Zinoviev were expelled from the Party. Trotsky was sent into internal exile in Alma Ata. He went from there to Turkey and on to France. While he was there he wrote 'A bulletin of the opposition'. This was advice to Stalin that he should create a new revolutionary international under Trotsky's leadership. Stalin ignored the advice. From France he went to Norway and then on to Mexico where he criticised the brutalities of Stalin's rule. He was murdered by one of Stalin's men in 1940. Zinoviev and Kamenev were eventually put on trial by Stalin in 1936. They were accused of terrorist crimes, found guilty and shot.

Stalin virtually secured his position at the Party Congress in 1927. Delegates agreed that no-one could vary from Party policy and that Party policy was defined by Stalin. While Stalin was willing to use the Party to catapult him to power, the other contenders were unwilling to use their power bases to take control. Trotsky didn't use the Red Army to take power in a military coup.

G

In January 1925 he was relieved of his post as Commissar of War without consultation with him and put in charge of electricity. The object was to isolate him from the Party by submerging him in routine work.
He made no protest, but plunged himself into his new work with all his old vigour.

From *Leon Trotsky, The Eternal Rebel,* by Ronald Seth, 1967

Tomsky, who controlled the trade unions, did not try to seize power through industrial action. They all felt that the Party should decide power and choose the leaders and, as we know, Stalin controlled the Party.

Stalin had used Bukharin, Tomsky, and Rykov (generally regarded as more right wing) against Zinoviev and Kamenev (the left opposition). Once he had got rid of Zinoviev and Kamenev, he was ready to dump Bukharin and the others. Bukharin, Rykov, and Tomsky were opposed to the brutal use of force against the peasants and to Stalin's policy of forced industrialisation. By 1929, Stalin had had enough of their opposition and criticism. He launched a campaign against them. They were publicly denounced in the press, forced, to apologise for their views and they lost their posts.

Stalin was now effectively dictator in Russia. For the next 25 years he ruled Russia with a rod of iron. Millions died because of his policies.

After the removal of his main political rivals, Stalin set about removing them from the history of the Revolution. The top photograph is from May 1920 and shows Lenin giving a speech. On the steps to his left are Trotsky and Kamenev. The bottom photograph is exactly the same picture, but Stalin has had Trotsky and Kamenev removed.

H **I**

Napoleon was a large rather fierce looking Berkshire boar, not much of a talker, but with a reputation for getting his own way …

Snowball was a more vivacious pig than Napoleon, quicker in speech and more inventive but was not considered to have the same depth of character …

Snowball also busied himself with organising the other animals into what he called animal committees. He was indefatigable in this …

Napoleon took no interest in Snowball's committees. He said that education of the young was more important than anything that could be done for those who were already grown up …

Jessie and Bluebell gave birth to nine sturdy puppies. Napoleon took them away from their mothers saying that he would make himself responsible for their education.

Snowball and Napoleon disagreed at every point where disagreement was possible. If one of them suggested sowing a bigger acreage with barley, the other was bound to demand a bigger acreage of oats.

Each one had his own following, and there were some violent debates. At the meetings Snowball often won over the majority by his brilliant speeches, but Napoleon was better at canvassing support for himself in between times. He was especially successful with the sheep. Of late the sheep had taken to bleating and often interrupted the meetings with this. It was noticed that they were especially likely to break into this at crucial moments in Snowball's speeches.

Snowball was full of plans for improvements and innovations. Napoleon produced no plans of his own, but said quietly that Snowball's would come to nothing and seemed to be biding his time.

Until now the animals had been about equally divided in their sympathies (about plans to build a windmill – Snowball for, Napoleon against) but in a moment Snowball's eloquence had carried them away.

Napoleon stood up and casting a peculiar sidelong look at Snowball uttered a high pitched whimper of a kind no one had heard him utter before.

At this there was a terrible baying sound outside, and nine enormous dogs wearing brass studded collars came bounding into the barn. They dashed straight for Snowball who only sprang from his place just in time to escape their snapping jaws. In a moment he was out of the door and they were after him. Too amazed and frightened to speak all the animals crowded through the door to watch the chase. Silent and terrified the animals crept back into the barn. In a moment the dogs came bounding back into the barn. At first no one had been able to imagine where these creatures came from but the problem was soon solved: they were the puppies whom Napoleon had taken away from their mothers and reared privately. Though not yet fully grown they were huge dogs and as fierce looking as wolves.

He announced that from now on the Sunday morning meetings would come to an end. In future all questions relating to the working of the farm would be settled by a special committee of pigs presided over by himself. There would be no more debates.

J From *Animal Farm* by George Orwell. This book is regarded by many as an accurate reflection of what happened in post-Revolutionary Russia. The account of the struggle for power between Napoleon (who represented Stalin) and Snowball (who represented Trotsky) is often used to gain an insight into the differences between Stalin and Trotsky.

1 Why did Stalin not want Lenin's will to be published?

2 Lenin criticized Stalin. Why do you think that in spite of this Stalin promoted hero-worship of Lenin?

3 What do Sources A, B, C and D tell us about Stalin's character?

4 What was the main issue that divided Stalin and Trotsky?

5 How did Stalin become so powerful?

6 i) What, according to Sources A and E, were Trotsky's strengths as a possible leader?
ii) Is there any evidence in Source F that it was his own fault that he lost power?

7 i) How do you explain the difference between Sources H and I?
ii) Does this mean that written sources are more reliable than photographs?

8 i) What image does Orwell give us of Stalin (Napoleon) and Trotsky (Snowball) in *Animal Farm*?
ii) Do you think that presenting it as a story about animals was effective?

9 Do you think Lenin, Source A, would have approved of the events that followed his death?

Essay: Describe how Stalin gained power.

5 Changes to agriculture

A modern state

Once Stalin had secured power he turned his attention to the economy. He wanted to modernize both agriculture and industry. Agricultural methods in the USSR were very primitive and levels of production were very low, despite the New Economic Policy. Stalin knew that more efficient farming methods and better production would give more capital (money) for industrial development. With increased mechanization, workers could also be transferred from the farms to the factories.

Foreign countries who were opposed to Communism would not send the USSR the capital that was needed for new factories and machinery. Stalin felt that he could get the capital through increased agricultural exports from the USSR. This could not be done, he asserted, from the twenty-five million small peasant holdings where the peasants just grew enough for themselves. The price the peasants got for their food from the State hardly covered the cost of producing it, so they just grew enough for themselves. Consequently, in 1928 the people in the towns went hungry.

▼ A

> What is the way out? The way out is to turn the small and scattered peasant farms into large united farms based on cultivation of the land in common … on the basis of a new higher technique. The way out is to unite the small and dwarf peasant farms gradually but surely, not by pressure but by example and persuasion into large farms based on common co-operative collective cultivation of the land … There is no other way out.

Stalin speaking to the Party Congress in 1927

Collectivization

Stalin set about modernizing farming through a policy known as collectivization. The peasants were required to join their farms together and work the land collectively as State employees. Large scale methods of production would be used with the aid of machinery. Each collective farm was to be supported by a motor tractor station where a pool of tractors were to be hired out to the collective. The peasants would work the collective under State control. The State could, therefore, control the supply of food to the cities and get enough foreign capital to industrialize. The first stage was collectivization by example. Peasants were encouraged to voluntarily join collectives. The policy didn't work. Few joined because the peasants wanted to own their own land. Therefore, very few collectives were set up.

▲ This photograph shows Government efforts to persuade peasants about the virtues of collectivization

A Government propaganda photograph showing women going off to work on the collective whilst their babies are looked after in the collective crèche

Reactions to collectivization

When exhortation didn't work, Stalin adopted a policy of forced collectivization. He began by trying to force food from the peasants. Young Party workers went round the country looking for food. They believed that the peasants were hoarding and hiding their food hoping thereby to force up the prices. Any food they found was confiscated for the Party. There were riots by the peasants against this forced requisitioning of food. Hundreds of party workers were assassinated. There were 1,400 reported cases of terrorist acts in 1928 alone.

There was even less food the following year, 1929. Food had to be rationed in the towns. Stalin decided to wage all out war on the peasants. Naturally he blamed them for the shortage of food and for frustrating his will. He was particularly venomous towards the richer peasants, the kulaks. He believed they were deliberately hoarding food and keeping the towns short. The kulaks, he said: 'are the sworn enemies of the collective farm movement. We are to eliminate them as a class … when the head is cut off one does not mourn for the hair.' Stalin began to use the language of war – the peasants, he claimed, had opened a second front, a livestock and grain front, against the State. To ensure that collectivization was successful he decided to smash the kulaks as a class.

B

For Stalin's propaganda machine, collectivization meant progress and technical advance. He wrote 'We are forging full speed ahead on the road to industrialization which leads to Socialism. We are leaving behind us our age old backward Russian past and when we motorize the USSR and put the peasant on a tractor, then let them try to catch us up – those respectable Capitalists with their much vaunted civilization.'

C

We must break down the resistance of the kulaks and deprive this class of its existence. We must eliminate the kulaks as a class. We must smash the kulaks … we must strike at the kulaks so hard as to prevent them rising to their feet again. We must annihilate them as a social class.

Stalin addressing the Party in 1929

I have made a tour of your territory and have had the opportunity to see for myself that your people are not seriously concerned to help the country to emerge from the grain crisis. You have had a bumper harvest … your grain surpluses this year are bigger than ever before. Yet the plan for collecting grain is not being fulfilled. Why? … Look at the kulak (rich peasant) farms: their barns and sheds are crammed with grain … You say the kulaks are demanding an increase in prices up to three times those fixed by the Government. The effect will be that our towns and the Red Army will be poorly supplied and threatened with hunger. Obviously we cannot allow that.

Stalin speaking to peasants in Siberia in 1928

No one ever defined what a kulak was. To Stalin it was the richer peasant. To the over enthusiastic Communist Party worker who wanted to carry out Stalin's policy, it was anyone who opposed collectivization. Being branded a kulak by a neighbour was often enough to ensure your expulsion from the village. In the beginning, Stalin talked of 5 or 6 million kulaks. Years later, when speaking to Churchill, he talked of 10 million.

Not all peasants opposed the collectives. This photograph shows a pro-collectivization demonstration from 1930. The banner reads: 'Liquidate the kulaks as a class'.

The decision to collectivize was taken in a hurry. No proper surveys of the country were carried out. This was to prove disastrous. To go from a system of privately owned small farms to State owned large farms and still ensure adequate food levels required careful planning. The Government wanted change at breakneck speed – in some areas they wanted complete collectivization in 18 months.

In this war against the peasants, the government had all the big battalions – they used the police, the secret police, and the army.

E

I am an old Bolshevik. I worked in the underground against the Tsar and then I fought in the Civil War. Did I do all that in order that I should now surround villages with machine guns and order my men to fire indiscriminately into crowds of peasants? Oh no, no!

Some of the army found their work distasteful. Here a Red Army commander remembers when he was sent to deal with a group of peasants who would not join the collective.

Nevertheless, the resistance of the peasants was greater than expected. The response of the peasants was generally hostile. Hostility became open resistance and rebellion. The peasants refused to donate any food to the Government, so they ate it in an orgy of feasting.

F

Stock was slaughtered every night in Gremyachy Log. Hardly had dusk fallen when the muffled, short bleats of sheep, the death squeal of pigs, or the lowing of calves could be heard. Both those who had joined the Kolkhoz (collective farm) and the individual farmers killed their stock. Bulls, sheep, pigs, even cows were slaughtered as well as cattle for breeding. The horned stock of Gremyachy was halved in two nights. The dogs began to drag entrails about the village. Cellars and barns were filled with meat. The co-operative sold about two hundred poods (about 36 lbs) of salt in two days, that had been lying in stock for eighteen months.

'Kill it's not ours any more ... Kill they'll take it for meat anyway ... Kill you won't get any meat in the Kolkhoz.' And they killed. They ate until they could eat no more. Young and old suffered from stomach ache. At dinner time tables groaned under boiled and roasted meat. At dinner time everyone had a greasy mouth, everyone hiccoughed as if at a wake. Everyone blinked like an owl, as if drunk from eating.

From *The Virgin Soil* by Mikhail Sholokov, 1977. This extract shows how a group of peasants reacted when they heard that their land was to be collectivized.

The results of collectivization

Likewise, to frustrate the Government, the peasants didn't plant anything for the following year. The new collectives were supposed to bring the advantages of the economies of scale with modernized farming methods. However, new tractors could not replace the slaughtered draught horses – half were killed. The figures are staggering: the USSR had 34 million horses in 1929 but only 17 million in 1933. In the same very short period 45% of its cattle and 60% of its sheep and goats were destroyed.

This was a very confusing time for the peasants. Source G shows this confusion.

G

'There was a time when we were neighbours. Now we are either very poor peasants or fairly wealthy peasants or kulaks. And we are supposed to have a class war. But it is other things that worry us … whoever heard of such a thing … to give up our land and cows etc. to work all the time and to divide everything with others? We, strangers are supposed to be like one family. Can we dull witted peasants make it go without scratching each other's faces? We won't be even sure of having enough to eat. No more potatoes of our own. Everything will be rationed out by orders. We shall be like mere serfs on the landlord's estate.'

The Communist among them then said: 'What hope is there for you if you remain on your individual pieces of land? From year to year as you increase in population you divide and sub-divide your strips of land. Under your present system nothing is ahead of you but ruin and starvation. You accuse us of making false promises. Let us see! Last year you got a school house and now aren't you glad your children can attend school?'

'The Kolkhoz is different' shouted the old man. The Communist replied: 'Of course it's different, different but better. Isn't it time you stopped thinking each one for himself? You kulaks, you will never accept the new order. You love to fatten on other people's blood. But we know how to deal with you. We will wipe you off the face of the earth.'

From *Red Bread,* by Hindus, 1931

Villagers who refused to co-operate with collectivization were forcibly removed from their villages. They were then herded into cattle trucks and dumped in the inhospitable north. Others were forced into labour camps where they provided slave labour for some of Stalin's difficult schemes.

Soon mass transportation of kulaks took place. In unheated railway cars thousands of peasants with their wives and children went east to the Urals, Kazakhstan, and Siberia. Many thousands died en route from hunger cold and disease. In winter, during a severe frost, a large group of Kulaks were taken in wagons three hundred kilometres away. One, unable to endure the crying of a baby sucking its mother's empty breast, grabbed the child and dashed its head against a tree.

An American correspondent set at two million the approximate number of those deported and exiled in 1929–1930. But the truth appears far worse if we realise that de-kulakisation continued without let up through the following years. Official figures vary between five and ten million people.

From *Let History Judge,* by R. Medvedev, 1971

When the peasants were evicted, the Party officials – often from the cities – had no idea how to farm. Crops were not harvested properly or seed sown in time.

There was chaos. With slaughtered cattle, bad harvesting, and burned crops there was famine again in the USSR. Millions starved. Stalin refused to accept international aid. Cannibalism appeared in some areas.

Because of the famine and the chaos, Stalin had to make concessions. He blamed his Party officials for excess of zeal, but he still had to make concessions. He allowed the peasants to own their own private plots plus a cow. The plot was to be small, no larger than two and half acres (about two football pitches). Yet these private plots were remarkably successful. As the peasants never believed in the collective, they devoted far more attention and effort to their private plots, which produced 52% of the USSR's potatoes and vegetables and 71% of its meat and milk in 1937.

J

The peasants soon discovered and have continued to discover innumerable small ways of 'getting their own back' on the collectives. In one farm, it is reported, the headman (who is a State-appointed official) bought 1,000 chickens out of the collective's profits. He gave them to the peasants and promised that they could keep half when the birds were fully grown, although the other half must be returned to the collective. Later when the headman inspected the returned birds he found that ninety per cent were roosters!

From *Stalin: man of steel,* by Elizabeth Roberts, 1968

Sources I and J show the attitude of the peasants to the collective.

A Russian cartoon illustrating the problem of the peasants on the collectives spending far more time and effort on their own private plots, than on the collective's land

Collectivization: an assessment

The scale of this operation is hard to imagine. Twenty-five million peasants were to be forced from their private farms onto huge collectives (about 400,000 of them). In just three months alone three million families were forced to join. In the teeth of fierce resistance the Government used terror and repression for three years to break the peasants. The full force of the State was used against them.

In 1987, Mikhail Gorbachev – who was then the leader of the USSR – criticised the Stalinist government of the 1930's. He condemned the wanton repressive measures of the 1930's as real crimes. He claimed that flagrant violations of the principles of collectivization occurred everywhere. No one knows how many Soviet citizens died. Estimates vary from 10 to 20 million. The Ukraine was the worst affected region. This was cruelly ironic because it was the most fertile part of the country. But the Ukrainians wanted more autonomy and Stalin claimed that it had the largest collection of kulaks. He used this excuse as an opportunity to end any opposition in the Ukraine. The borders were sealed – no one could leave. Some historians suggest that Stalin purposely caused the famine in the Ukraine. It is estimated that 5 million Ukrainians alone died in this man made famine.

Stalin had in a ruthless way smashed the richer peasants, the kulaks. The price was intolerably high. He also used this as another opportunity to break down the religious commitment of the peasants. Using the excuse that the peasants were hoarding food in the churches, he forcibly closed thousands of churches, thus trying to break the spirit of the peasants. However, he did not achieve his principal aim of increasing agricultural exports to earn foreign capital. The levels of pre-collectivization agricultural production were not reached again until the 1950's. We have seen already how the tiny privately-owned plots were more popular and productive than the collectives.

In one sense Stalin gained more control over the peasants – in 1932 internal passports were introduced in the USSR, so the peasants could not leave the collectives. On the other hand, Stalin never convinced the peasants of the advantages of Communism. Collectives did not increase Party membership. The peasants remained understandably suspicious.

In strict statistical terms Stalin was successful. In 1928, only 2% of the farms were collectivized. By 1932, 62% were collectivized.

We have some insight into Stalin's attitude to the whole collectivization episode in a conversation he had with Churchill during the Second World War.

'Tell me' I asked 'have the stresses of this war been as bad to you personally as carrying through the policy of the collective farms?'

This subject immediately roused Stalin. 'Oh no' he said, 'the collective farm policy was a terrible struggle'.

'I thought you would have found it bad', said I, 'because you were not dealing with a few score thousands of aristocrats or big landowners, but with millions of small men'.

'Ten millions', he said holding up his hands. 'It was fearful. Four years it lasted. It was absolutely necessary for Russia, if we were to avoid periodic famines, to plough the land with tractors. We must mechanize our agriculture. When we gave tractors to the peasants they were all spoiled in a few months. Only the collective farms with workshops could handle tractors. We took the greatest trouble to explain it all to the peasants. It was no use arguing with them. After you have said all you can to a peasant he says he must go home and consult his wife. After he has talked it over he always answers that he doesn't want the collective farm, and he would rather do without the tractors.'

'These are what you would call the kulaks?' I asked.

'Yes', he said, but he did not repeat the word.

After a pause he said 'it was all very bad and difficult – but necessary'.

From *The Second World War,* by Winston Churchill

Fascinated peasants examine the first tractor to arrive on the collective farm

1 What did Stalin mean when he said, 'The struggle for bread is the struggle for Socialism?'

2 In Source A, how did Stalin propose to increase food production?

3 How did Stalin's attitude change between Source A and Source B?

4 How did the peasants feel about collectivization?

5 Why was Stalin so determined to 'smash the kulaks' in Source C?

6 What do Sources D, E, G and H, tell us about the treatment of the kulaks?

7 What is the point being made in Source I?

8 If more food was needed and collectivization was the answer, then was Stalin justified in using any means necessary?

9 What possible reasons were behind Stalin's refusal to accept aid from other countries when his own people were starving?

10 What does the process of collectivization tell us about Stalin as the leader of the USSR?

Essay:

i) Collectivization was 'all very bad and difficult – but necessary.' Is this a fair assessment?

ii) Propaganda was an important tool used by Stalin. Prepare a propaganda statement in support of collectivization.

6 Changes to industry

A modern industrial nation

Stalin wanted to transform the USSR from a backward agricultural country to a modern industrial state. This change was to be as revolutionary as the Revolution of 1917. It was an extraordinarily ambitious project. Stalin felt that the USSR had to modernize, or the western Capitalist countries would defeat her. The Socialist revolution, he believed, could only be saved by rapid industrialization. Industrial might was necessary for national strength and for military might. Industrial strength was the key to survival in a modern Capitalist world.

In short, Stalin wanted to modernize in case the USSR was attacked by the West. Consequently, certain types of industry were emphasized, such as steel and coal, and others, such as textiles, were overlooked. According to Stalin: 'the Red Army would not fight with leather and textiles, but with metal.'

A

One feature of the history of old Russia was the continual beatings she suffered because of her backwardness. She was beaten by the Mongol Khans. She was beaten by the Turkish boyars. She was beaten by the Swedish feudal lords. She was beaten by the Polish and Lithuanian gentry. She was beaten by the British and French Capitalists. She was beaten by the Japanese barons. All beat her because of her backwardness, political backwardness, industrial backwardness, agricultural backwardness. They beat her because to do so was profitable and could be done with impunity. Such is the law of the exploiters – to beat the backward and the weak. It is the jungle law of Capitalism. You are backward, you are weak – therefore you are wrong; hence you can be beaten and enslaved. This is why we must no longer lag behind.

In the past we had no fatherland, nor could we have one. But now that we have overthrown Capitalism and power is in our hands, in the hands of the people, we have a fatherland, and we will defend its independence. Do we want our Socialist fatherland to be beaten and to lose its independence? If you do not want this to happen, you must put an end to backwardness in the shortest possible time and you must develop genuine Bolshevik tempo in building up our Socialist system of economy. There is no other way.

This is why Lenin said on the eve of the October Revolution: 'Either perish, or overtake and outstrip the advanced Capitalist countries.'

It is time to adopt a new policy, a policy adapted to the present times – the policy of interfering in everything. If you are a factory manager then interfere in all the affairs of the factory, look into everything, let nothing escape you, learn and learn again. Bolsheviks must master technique. It is time Bolsheviks themselves became experts. In the period of reconstruction technique decides everything. We are fifty to one hundred years behind, we must catch up in ten years or they will beat us.

From a speech to factory managers in February 1931 in which Stalin explained why industrialization was necessary

The Plans

The country was to be modernized by a series of Five Year Plans. The First Plan emphasised heavy industry, especially iron and steel. Tractor plants had a high priority, partly to replace the slaughtered draught horses on the farms but also because they could easily be converted into tank factories in the event of war. Impossibly high goals were set for each industry and for each factory.

Output was to be doubled in five years in iron and steel production, in electricity, chemicals, and engineering (for example, 170,000 tractors were to be produced). After some initial success, these early targets were increased and the First Five Year Plan was ordered to be completed in four not five years. The planning was done by a new Government department called Gosplan. They set targets for growth in each industry. They planned new towns, new roads, new railways, a new landscape, a new Soviet Union. Many of these new towns and industrial centres were to be built beyond the Ural Mountains, beyond the reach of a foreign invasion. They had a huge task: to transform the world's largest country – one sixth of the surface of the earth – from a backward farming country to an industrial giant, the equal of the USA. New workers were needed for the new mines and factories. Many came from the farms. Many of these were displaced peasants, displaced in the drive to collectivize the farms.

A poster from 1928 during the First Five Year Plan. It says: 'Industrialization is the path to Socialism'.

B

First Five Year Plan: targets and achievements

Item	1927 (actual)	1932/3 (plan)	1932/3 (actual)
National Income (milliard roubles)	24.4	49.7	45.5
Gross industrial production (milliard roubles):	18.3	43.2	43.3
a) Producer's goods	6.0	18.1	23.1
b) Consumer's goods	12.3	25.1	20.2
Gross agricultural production (in milliard roubles)	13.1	25.8	16.6
Electricity (milliard kWh)	5.05	22.0	13.4
Coal (million tons)	35.4	75.0	64.3
Oil (million tons)	11.7	22.0	21.4
Pig iron (million tons)	3.3	10.0	6.2
Steel (million tons)	4.0	10.4	5.9
Total employed labour force (millions)	11.3	15.8	22.8

C

Rural and urban population, 1920–1939		
Year	Rural population (millions)	Urban population (millions)
1920	110.0	20.8
1923	119.9	21.6
1926	120.7	26.3
1929	126.7	27.6
1931	128.5	33.6
1933	125.4	40.3
1939	114.5	56.1

The Central Government took over complete control of the economy. The private sector of the NEP was brought to an end. Shopkeepers, barbers, cafe owners, and tradesmen were forced out of business or into collectives. They were criticized in the press, harassed by the authorities, and many were arrested. Industrialization was being used (like collectivization of agriculture) not only to modernize, but also to complete the Socialist revolution. This could only be done, they believed, by the worker – in town and country – working for the State and ending private business of any sort. The planners were intent on producing more than the West. They intended to build the newest and biggest industry, not only the equal of the West, but better than it. Whole new areas that had never previously even seen any motor cars were developed into some of the largest industrial complexes in the world. This fundamentally altered the economic map of the USSR.

The First Plan: a success

In 1932 Stalin announced that the First Five Year Plan was a great success. They had met their targets nine months early. This was not completely true. However, there were considerable successes: iron and steel production had doubled; and electricity generation had trebled. But the wildly optimistic goals were not achieved. Only 51,000 of the planned 170,000 tractors were made, and steel production

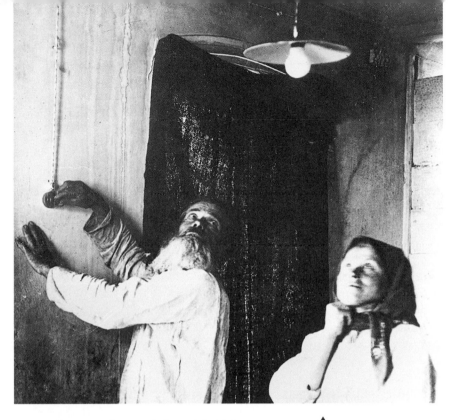

was still 40% short of the 100,000 tons target. Even though Stalin wasn't entirely truthful when he said that the 1928 targets had been 'overfulfilled with maximum overfulfillment', the foundations for a successful industrial economy had been laid.

However, the planners and the managers of the new factories had met with problems. Very few of the Soviet workers had the technical skills necessary for industrial work. Many were semi-literate because on average they had spent only three years in junior school. In some factories they were using their fingers to measure equipment. In others, expensive equipment lay idle as no one knew how to mend it when it broke. As many of the new industrial workers were peasants, they were unused to the strict routine of factory life. They often found it difficult to adjust to the regularity of daily work as they were used to farming routines which are dictated by weather and seasons, not by a factory siren. Sometimes new conveyor belts lay idle while tractors were made by craftsmen in the factory in the traditional skilled craftsman's fashion.

Despite these problems, the Government went ahead with the Second Five Year Plan in 1932.

▲ Peasants in the village of Bryansk Gubernia trying out their first electric light bulb in 1928

The Second Plan

Second Five Year Plan: targets and achievements			
Item	1933 (actual)	1937 (plan)	1937 (actual)
National Income (milliard roubles)	45.5	100.0	96.0
Gross industrial production (milliard roubles):	43.3	92.0	95.0
a) Producer's goods	23.1	45.0	55.2
b) Consumer's goods	20.2	47.2	40.3
Gross agricultural production (milliard roubles)	16.6	36.0	20.1
Electricity (milliard kWh)	13.4	38.0	36.2
Coal (million tons)	64.3	152.5	128.0
Oil (million tons)	21.4	46.8	28.5
Pig Iron (million tons)	6.2	16.0	14.5
Steel (million tons)	5.9	17.0	17.7
Employed labour force (millions)	22.8	28.9	26.9
Average money wage (roubles per annum)	1427.0	1755.0	3047.0
Retail price index (1933=100)	100.0	65.0	180.0
Volume of retail trade (1933=100)	100.0	250.6	150.0

Far more realistic targets than the First Plan were set. As the skilled workers were becoming more competent, they were more efficient at seeing the Plans implemented more effectively. This Plan promised to concentrate more on consumer goods, and on getting the quality of the goods right. But as the threat of Hitler's Germany became more apparent, targets were changed to prepare the country for war. The promise of more consumer goods was abandoned. From 1934 onwards, far more was spent on military preparation. Before and during the war factories were moved eastwards, away from Germany.

By the end of the Second Five Year Plan, the Soviet Union had surpassed Germany in industrial output and was second only to the USA. It had become a major industrial power. What had taken other countries fifty to one hundred years to achieve had been accomplished in little over a decade. However, what was the cost for the workers?

The impact of industrialization

To ensure that their targets were reached, the Government went back on their more idealistic Communist ideals. All workers had targets set for them. Their wages depended on them achieving these targets.

Higher wages were offered for better and more skilled work.

As the labour force wasn't educated, and an industrial society needs its workers to be educated, a massive education programme was undertaken. Initially, Stalin attracted highly educated and skilled workers from the West by offering very high wages. But this was no long term solution. Education had to expand. New colleges, schools, and universities were built. Everyone was to receive at least elementary education. Thousands of teachers, scientists, and engineers were trained. These new professionals, and the highly skilled (highly paid) workers, together with the factory managers, provided a new elite in Soviet Russia.

Women in Tashkent being taught to read and write in 1928

▼

Hard work was rewarded with medals; and there were also subsidized holidays to the Black Sea and to Moscow. The highest achievement was the Order of Lenin, reserved for the best workers. All were encouraged to be like the heroic Stakhanov. He was a miner who surpassed his quota of ten tons, in fact he cut an awesome 102 tons. However, the full story is less heroic. Stakhanov had a team of miners helping him; he had the most modern equipment; and he worked on a rich seam of coal. Nevertheless he became a national hero. To help the workers emulate Stakhanov, other model workers were honoured. Many young workers were convinced in an idealistic way of Stalin's plans for modernizing the country. These shock workers tried to urge the others on to greater effort and higher productivity. Anyone who opposed this industrial policy was accused of defeatism. These shock workers were not popular and in some cases they were lynched.

The Government was too autocratic (dictatorial) to rely solely on the inducements of medals, holidays, and higher wages to ensure efficiency and higher productivity. Fines were imposed for lateness and bad workmanship. Persistent offenders were imprisoned and sometimes shot. Sunday was no longer guaranteed as a rest day. Added to these restrictive work practices, the workers had to endure poor living conditions. Real wages halved from 1928 to 1933. Towns grew too quickly to absorb the new workers from the farms. Sanitation and housing were poor. Several families often crowded together to live in a single room. Understandably problems grew – juvenile delinquency, crime, and alcoholism were common. Conditions were even worse on the new industrial sites east of the Urals.

▶ Alexei Stakhanov is shown explaining his method of working to fellow miners in 1935

One of the new industrial sites built by Stalin during the Five Year Plans. This is Magnitogorsk, which was built beyond the Ural Mountains. It was the largest mining plant in the world. The workers had to live in tents and share beds as they worked on shifts.

ОРУЖИЕМ МЫ ДОБИЛИ ВРАГА ТРУДОМ МЫ ДОБУДЕМ ХЛЕБ ВСЕ ЗА РАБОТУ, ТОВАРИЩИ!

E

The Bolsheviks always encouraged women and men to work together in the interests of the new Socialist state. This poster, dating from after the Civil War, reads: 'With our weapons we have routed the enemy; with our labour we shall get bread. All to work, Comrades!' Stalin's Five Year Plans continued this policy.

Slave labour from the labour camps being used to build the Baltic Canal in 1933

The most difficult work was done by forced labour. Projects like the Moscow Underground and the White Sea Canal were completed by workers from the labour camps. Stalin had his opponents locked up in labour camps all over the Soviet Union.

Women were encouraged to work in the new factories to ensure that the targets for the Five Year Plans were reached. However, the number of deserted wives grew with the easing of the divorce laws. Because of this, and the concern over the slow population growth, divorce became harder to obtain in 1936. Motherhood was now encouraged: 'A woman who has not known the joy of motherhood has not yet realised the greatness of her calling.' During the war years, medals were awarded to those mothers with large families, and bachelors and spinsters were taxed.

G

At this factory milk station, female workers have filled bottles with their breast milk before they start their shift. This prepared milk can then be fed to their babies in the factory crèche without the need for the mothers to stop working on the factory floor.

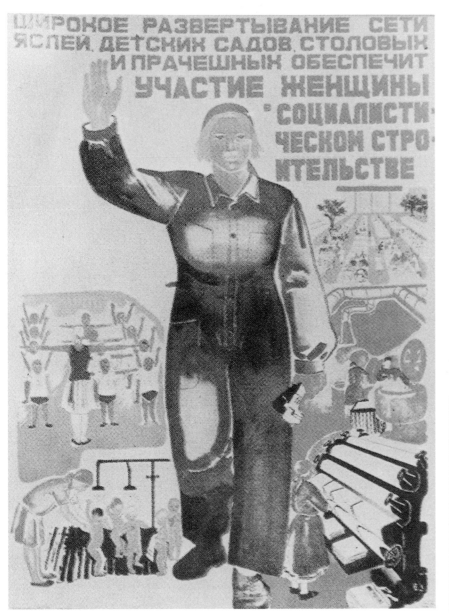

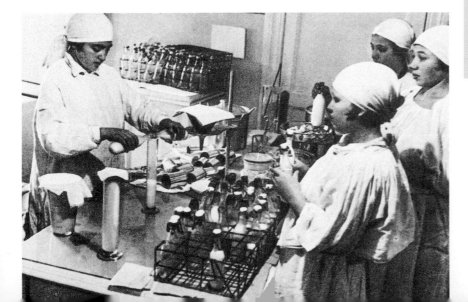

Industrialization: an assessment

Some historians regard the industrialization of the Soviet Union as Stalin's greatest achievement. When one considers how backward the country was; how large it was; and the recovery that was needed after the horrors of the Civil War, then the achievement is remarkable.

Stalin had improved industrial production by ten times since 1914. The Soviet Union was, by the outbreak of the Second World War, second only to the USA. Most important of all, it was able to withstand the German onslaught in 1941 and had the industrial resources to help defeat Hitler.

H

F This poster from 1931 is encouraging women to work in the new factories, but also to have children. 'The wide development of a network of crèches, kindergartens, canteens, and laundries will ensure the participation of women in Socialist construction.'

Comparative statistics of Russia with the other great powers 1913 and 1940

1913

Country	Pig Iron (million tons)	Steel (million tons)	Coal (million tons)
Russia	4.8	5.2	36.0
USA	30.9	31.3	509.9
UK	10.3	7.7	287.0
Germany	19.3	18.3	190.0
France	5.2	4.7	40.8

1940

Country	Pig Iron (million tons)	Steel (million tons)	Coal (million tons)
Russia	14.9	18.4	164.6
USA	31.9	47.2	359.0
UK	6.7	10.3	227.0
Germany	18.3	22.7	186.0
France	6.0	6.1	45.5

An overview of the Russian (and Soviet) economy 1913–1953

Product	1913	1921	1928	1933	1940	1945	1953
Agricultural							
Grain (million tons)	86	36	73	69	95	75	83
Cows (millions)	29	25	29	19	28	23	25
Pigs (millions)	23	13	19	10	27	11	29
Industrial							
Electrical power (billion kwh)	2	0.5	5	16	48	43	119
Crude oil (million tons)	9	4	12	22	31	19	48
Coal (million tons)	29	9	35	76	165	149	301
Steel (million tons)	4	0.2	4	7	18	12	34
Trucks (millions)	0	0	0.7	4	14	7	24
Tractors (millions)	0	0	0.1	7	3	0.7	10
Consumer							
Automobiles (millions)	0	0	0	1	0.5	0.5	6
Washing machines (millions)	0	0	0	0	0	0	0.5
Cameras (millions)	0	0	0	3	35	0	46
Radio sets (millions)	0	0	0	3	16	1.5	129
Shoes (million pairs)	60	28	58	90	211	63	238

1 What reasons did Stalin give in Source A for the need for industrialization?

2 What does the evidence in Sources B, C and D tell us about the effect of the Five Year Plans?

3 Did the Second Five Year Plan make the USSR a major industrial nation?

4 Why weren't Stakhanovites popular with everyone?

5 How could Stalin have used the statistics in Sources H and I to prove the success of his policies?

6 Do these statistics prove that everyone in the USSR was better off as a result of Stalin's policies?

7 What are the strengths and weaknesses of statistics as historical evidence?

8 Why was it so important to the Communists that the USSR should produce more goods than the West?

9 What evidence is there in this chapter that there was little individual freedom in the USSR?

10 What was the connection between industrialization and defence?

11 What were some of the social problems in the industrial towns?

12 Explain the reasons behind Stalin's attitude to divorce and motherhood.

13 What different roles of women in the USSR are shown in Source G?

14 Using the information throughout this chapter explain what was meant by the phrase, 'Industrialization is the path to Socialism'.

Essay: How did Stalin's economic policies change the USSR?

7 The Reign of Terror

The labour camps

This is the story of an horrific period in the Soviet Union. Stalin got rid of all opposition real or imaginary in the most chillingly brutal fashion. After four years of Terror, he was the only one of the original Bolshevik leaders left. Everyone was afraid that they or one of their family would be arrested and sent to forced labour camps, or shot in the back of the head by the secret police. The death penalty even included twelve year olds.

The sources in this chapter are from *The Gulag Archipelago* by Alexander Solzhenitsyn. He wrote it from his own experiences of imprisonment and forced labour. He tells the tales of numerous victims of Stalin's Terror and of Soviet labour camps and prisons. He wanted to tell the story of a vicious period that killed, ruined, and deformed millions of people. At the beginning of the book he says: 'In this book there are no fictitious persons nor fictitious events. People and places are named with their own names. If they are identified by initials instead of names it is for personal considerations. If they are not named at all it is only because human nature has failed to preserve their names. But it all took place just as it is here described.'

The purges begin

Stalin began purging the Party in the early 1930's. In 1930 he removed 30% of the secretariat from their posts. People were put on trial – as we saw in the last chapter – to ensure that the Five Year Plans were successful. Foreign specialists were made scapegoats. Usually the toughest penalty for these industrial crimes was deportation.

Stalin faced considerable criticism for his handling of industrialization and collectivization. His wife told him he was bringing famine and ruin to the country. He would not listen. She committed suicide. His son also tried to kill himself. Some of the other leaders were also critical of his policies. They were especially critical of the low living standards that the workers had to endure, and of the excesses of forced collectivization. The most damning criticism emerged in a 200 page document in which Stalin was called: 'the evil genius of the Revolution, who, motivated by a personal desire for power and revenge, brought the Revolution to the verge of ruin'. The document, written by Ryutin, called for Trotsky and others to be reinstated. Stalin's reaction was to call for the execution of Ryutin, but the Politburo refused to sanction Ryutin's execution. So, up to 1932 and 1933 there was opposition to Stalin and he wasn't in total control, yet.

In 1933, Stalin set up a purging commission to purge all undesirables from the Party. The drunks, the undisciplined, the bourgeois, and the hypocrites were to be expelled. This purge (clearing out) of thousands of members concentrated on ordinary Party members. This was to change in 1934 after the murder of Kirov.

Kirov was the party boss in Leningrad. He counselled moderation in industrialization and collectivization policy. At the 17th Party Congress, in 1934, many felt that Kirov was as popular as Stalin. He was seen as a possible rival to Stalin and some had earlier asked him to oppose Stalin as leader. He had argued and disagreed with Stalin, for instance he had asked for more rations for the poorly fed workers. However, he was murdered in

1934. Later his personal bodyguard was killed in a car accident, so he was unable to give evidence at the trial of the assassin. No one knows if Stalin ordered Kirov's murder. But he used it as an opportunity to consolidate his power by ridding himself of all opposition.

The earlier purge had concentrated on ordinary Party members. Stalin now set about getting rid of the most senior Communists. There were 1,966 delegates at the 17th Party Congress in 1934, and of these 1,108 were arrested.

Arrest by the NKVD (the successor to the CHEKA) was a terrifying experience, as this extract from *The Gulag Archipelago* reveals.

And nothing is sacred in a search. During the arrest of the locomotive engineer, Inochin, a tiny coffin stood in his room containing the body of his newly dead child. The police dumped the child's body out of the coffin and searched it. They shake sick people out of their beds and they unwind bandages to search beneath them ... In 1937 a woman came to the reception room of the NKVD to ask what she should do about the unfed unweaned infant of a neighbour who had been arrested. They took her and tossed her into a cell.

Political opponents

Out of the 139 members of the Central Committee, 98 were arrested. Most of these were shot. Of Lenin's original Politburo of 7, only one remained. That was Stalin.

Stalin's newly reorganised secret police force, the NKVD, were ordered to find and arrest all traitors. They claimed that much of Leningrad where Kirov had been the popular Party boss were disloyal. 30,000 ordinary citizens of Leningrad were rounded up and sent to work in forced labour camps. These camps were in the inhospitable regions of Siberia and the Arctic north. Some estimates suggest that a quarter of the population of Leningrad ended up in labour camps (gulags).

B

In 1932, at one time 265 prisoners were awaiting execution in Leningrad's Kristy prison alone. (This is the testimony of B who brought food to the cells of the prisoners condemned to be shot). And during the whole year it would certainly seem that more than 1000 were shot in Kristy alone ...

It is also believed that a quarter of Leningrad was purged – cleaned out – from 1934 to 1955. Let this be disproved by those who have the exact statistics and are willing to publish them ... Where is that special archive we might be able to penetrate in order to read the figures? There is none. Therefore, we dare only mention these figures mentioned in rumours that were quite fresh in 1939 to 1940, coming from high ranking secret policemen who had been arrested (and they really knew). They said that during 1937/1938 half a million political prisoners had been shot.

From *The Gulag Archipelago,* by Alexander Solzhenitsyn

The most famous Bolsheviks (still seen by Stalin as potential rivals to his power) were submitted to staged show trials. Former colleagues of Lenin, who had planned and executed the Revolution, were accused of fantastically unbelievable plots. They were alleged to be conspiring with Trotsky to overthrow Stalin. The intention of these trials was to ridicule these old Bolsheviks before executing them. Kamenev, Zinoviev and others were accused of being 'a gang of murderers, wreckers and spies'; they were called agents of the Fascist Trotsky; they were accused of causing train collisions in the USSR; they were called terrorists responsible for blowing up mines and factories; they poisoned workers; they intended to reimpose the landlords; to re-establish Capitalism; and they wanted, according to the prosecutor, to break up the USSR by giving the Ukraine to the Germans and the Far East to Japan.

Some of the accused were so broken that they killed themselves before their trial. Many of the trials were remarkable not only for the fantastically trumped up charges but also because the accused confessed to committing these crimes. We should remember that they had been tortured; brutal threats were made against their families; and they were promised falsely lenient sentences.

C

A further method used to extract a confession was to blackmail your love for your family.

They would threaten to arrest everyone you loved. Sometimes this would be done with sound effects. Your wife has already been arrested but her further fate depends on you. They are questioning her in the next room – just listen! And through the wall you can actually hear a woman weeping and screaming. (After all they all sound alike; you're hearing it through a wall. Sometimes they simply play a recording of the voice of a typical wife).

Or they give you a letter to read and the handwriting is exactly like hers. 'I renounce you! After the filth they have told me about you I don't need you any more.'

(And since such wives do exist in our country and such letters as well, you are left to ponder in your heart: Is that the kind of wife she really is?).

From *The Gulag Archipelago,* by Alexander Solzhenitsyn

While the show trials were in progress the Party newspaper, *Pravda*, conducted its own trial of the accused on its front page. They condemned the accused, calling them 'spies and traitors of their country'. They called on the authorities to shoot them. The chief prosecutor called the accused 'mad dogs of Capitalism'. They were shot.

The Terror spreads

Soon the Terror reached beyond the Party. It reached everywhere. No village, no home could escape, not even Stalin's own family could escape. Cousins and in-laws were victims of the Terror. Even his closest advisor was arrested and shot. Millions of ordinary Soviet citizens were affected by the purges. Anyone could receive a knock on the door in the middle of the night and be dragged away by the secret police. The country seemed to go crazy.

D

A woman was going home late one night ... she passed some people working to free a truck that had got stuck. It turned out to be full of corpses – hands and legs stuck out from beneath the canvas. The men at the truck wrote down her name. The next day she was arrested. The interrogator asked her what she had seen. She told him truthfully. She was sentenced to ten years for anti-Soviet agitation.

From *The Gulag Archipelago,* by Alexander Solzhenitsyn

Neighbours denounced each other to the police. People were encouraged to report the 'crimes' of their neighbours and colleagues. They did. Denunciation brought arrest and removal from one's job. This opportunity for advancement may be one reason why people were willing to denounce their colleagues. Once arrested they were forced into some confession, which included denouncing other colleagues. Brutal interrogation methods were designed to break down your resistance. Many of those arrested simply had the confessions beaten out of them.

These confessions grew and grew until the secret police had files on half the urban population in the Soviet Union. Any excuse was used to arrest people as Source E shows.

A district party conference was under way in Moscow Province. At the conclusion of the conference a tribute to Comrade Stalin was called for. The small hall echoed with stormy applause rising to an ovation: for three minutes, four minutes, five minutes … The older people were panting from exhaustion. The applause went on six, seven, eight minutes. The NKVD were watching to see who quit first.

The director of the local paper factory, aware of all the falsity, sat down after eleven minutes. And, oh what a miracle took place, where had all the enthusiasm gone? To a man everyone else stopped dead and sat down.

That same night the paper factory director was arrested. His interrogator told him 'Don't ever be the first to stop applauding '.

From *The Gulag Archipelago,* by Alexander Solzhenitsyn

The next of kin of the arrested and executed seldom knew what had happened to them. The authorities did not tell them that their loved ones had been executed, rather that they had been: 'sentenced to exile without the right to send or to receive letters.' The families continued to hope that they were alive, even if they were in the hated Siberian gulags. No one can know precisely how many were executed in the Terror and how many were left languishing in the labour camps. Conditions in the prisons and in the labour camps were difficult to endure and many died there.

The country had gone crazy. Bizarre charges were made against these ordinary innocent people. If an historian was arrested, he or she was likely to be charged with terrorism, others with a crime called Trotskyism. They even had a crime called 'being a member of an accused family'. If one of your family were arrested you were all potentially guilty. It turned the dictum 'innocent until proven guilty' on its head. All aspects of Soviet society had to be controlled. Stalin wanted total control (totalitarianism).

In 1938 Ivanor Razannik found 140 prisoners in a cell intended for 25 – with toilets so overburdened that prisoners were taken to the toilet only once a day, sometimes at night. And the same was true of their outdoor walk as well. It was Ivanor Razannik who in the Lubyanka reception kennel calculated that for weeks at a time there were three persons for each square yard of floor space (just as an experiment try to fit three people into that space!).

In this kennel there was neither ventilation nor a window, and the prisoners' body heat and breathing raised the temperature to 40°C or 45°C. Their naked bodies were pressed against one another and they got eczema from one another's sweat. They sat like that for weeks at a time and were given neither fresh air nor water – except for gruel and tea in the morning …

A newly arrested prisoner was without explanation given a spade and ordered to dig a pit the exact dimensions of a grave. When the prisoner had dug a pit deeper than his waist they ordered him to stop and sit down on the bottom. One guard kept watch over several such pits. They kept the accused in this desert with no protection from the Mongolian sun and with no warm clothing against the cold of the night, but no tortures: why waste time on tortures? The ration they gave was three and a half ounces of bread per day and one glass of water. Lieutenant Chulpenyev spent a month imprisoned in this way. Within ten days he was swarming with lice. After fifteen days he was summoned to interrogation for the first time …

The prison doctor was the interrogator's right hand man. The beaten prisoner would come to on the floor only to hear the doctor's voice: 'you can continue, the pulse is normal'. After a prisoner's five days and nights in a punishment cell the prison doctor inspects the frozen, naked body and says: 'you can continue'. If a prisoner is beaten to death, he signs the death certificate 'Cirrhosis of the liver', or 'Coronary occlusion'.

He gets an urgent call to a dying prisoner in a cell and he takes his time. And whoever behaves differently is not kept on (as a doctor) in the prison.

From *The Gulag Archipelago,* by Alexander Solzhenitsyn

The location of the labour camps in the Soviet Union

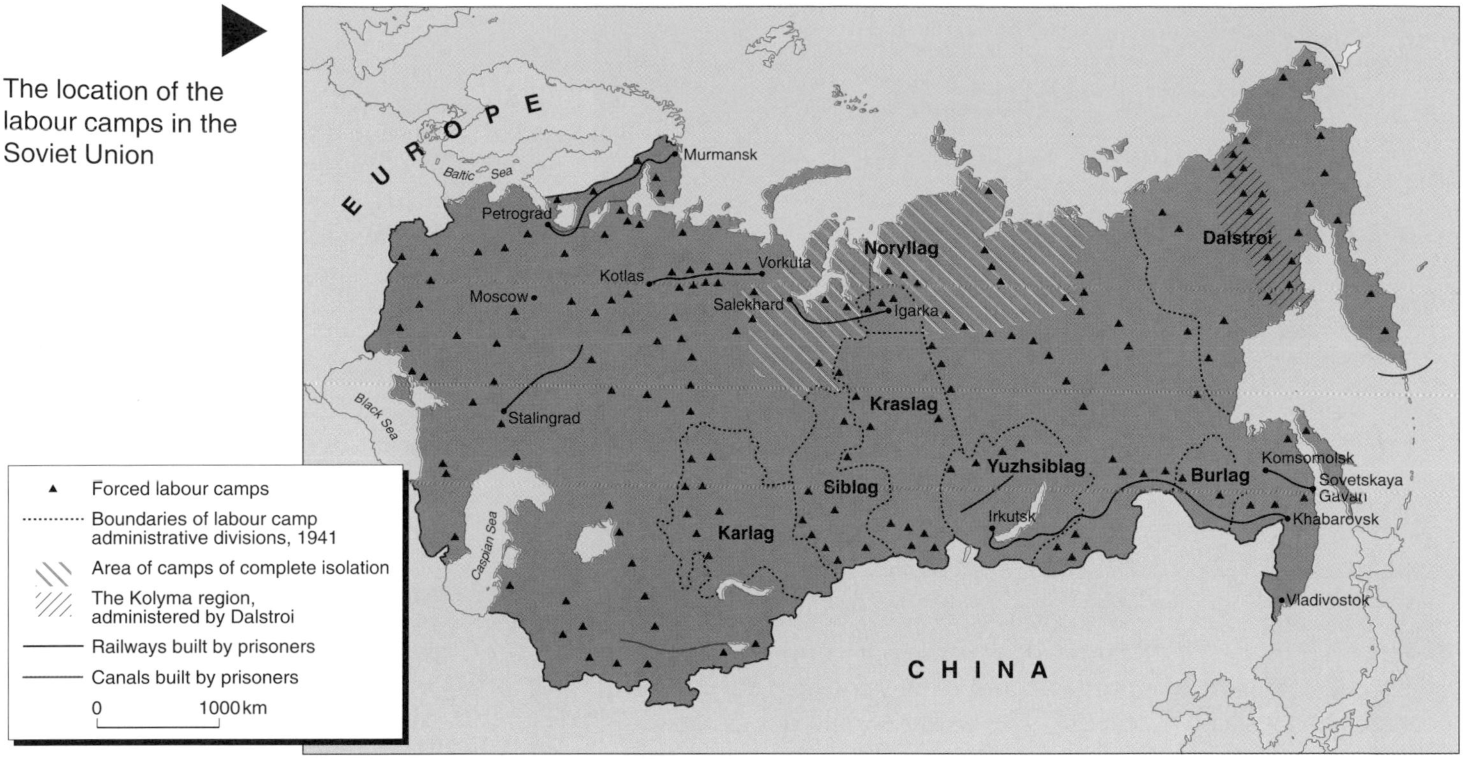
EUROPE
Baltic Sea
Murmansk
Petrograd
Moscow
Kotlas
Vorkuta
Salekhard
Igarka
Noryllag
Dalstroi
Black Sea
Stalingrad
Kraslag
Yuzhsiblag
Burlag
Komsomolsk
Sovetskaya Gavan
Khabarovsk
Siblag
Karlag
Caspian Sea
Irkutsk
Vladivostok
CHINA
Forced labour camps
Boundaries of labour camp administrative divisions, 1941
Area of camps of complete isolation
The Kolyma region, administered by Dalstroi
Railways built by prisoners
Canals built by prisoners
0 1000km

Cultural control

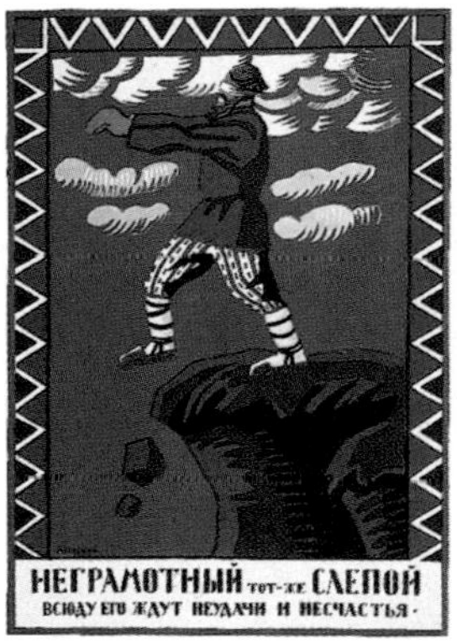
НЕГРАМОТНЫЙ тот-же СЛЕПОЙ
ВСЮДУ ЕГО ЖДУТ НЕУДАЧИ И НЕСЧАСТЬЯ

A literacy campaign poster from 1921. The text reads: 'To be illiterate is to be blind – on all sides lurk failure and unhappiness'.

When the Bolsheviks took power, they realised that the majority of the population were illiterate. In order to create a modern industrialized society, they needed an educated workforce. Their first aim, therefore, was to achieve universal primary education as quickly as possible. They launched a massive propaganda campaign to encourage greater literacy. One poster compared an illiterate person with a blind man heading for a cliff. Within ten years they had almost achieved this objective.

Education was also the key to ensuring that the whole population became Communists. They tried to encourage the children to think and believe in a collectivist way and thereby to develop a new Socialist citizen. Under Stalin, teachers and professors who were suspect in their teaching were arrested. Stalin sought to control what people were taught and what they were allowed to think.

Even though the new Bolshevik regime after 1917 wanted to control writers in Russia, and ensure that what was written praised Communism, they were not very effective in the 1920's. Writers were allowed to write more or less what they wanted, unless it was regarded as counter-Revolutionary. The well known writers continued, for a number of years, to write as they had done before the Revolution.

Stalin gradually restricted creative freedom. Literature was controlled by a Communist Writers Union, who allowed the Party bosses to intervene and decide what should be published. Literature reflected Stalin's wishes and his goals: books praised the ordinary worker working heroically for the good of the Soviet state. Later, when the emphasis in the Five Year Plans was on the specialist engineer and scientist, then, sure enough, the loyal Communist writers made them the heros of their novels. Other novels praised collectivization and painted an image of happy farmers which ignored the horror, the internal Civil War, and the millions of deaths. Writers had become a mere publicity machine for the State.

Art and music also had to have a Socialist message. It had to be 'realistic'. Failure by the artist to provide the correct Socialist propaganda message led to arrest and the labour camp. Even folk singers were encouraged to write and perform songs praising the success of the Five Year Plans. This turned the style of folk singers on its head – they usually sang of the honest experiences of the ordinary man.

G

Well fed and happy peasants at a feast on the collective farm. Artists, too, were used to reinforce the Socialist message.

This policy became known as Socialist Realism. It was the duty of the writer to be optimistic and to thereby help Socialism to develop. The writer should not express any doubt or confusion. To be published you had to belong to the Union of Soviet Writers, and they saw it as their duty to ensure that the right attitude was in all books. The greatest praise was reserved for Stalin, who was described as a superman hero – the inspiration of everyone's life. Those who were more independent minded either kept quiet and wrote nothing or ended up in the camps.

Several dozen young people got together for some kind of musical evening which had not been authorised ahead of time by the police. They listened to music and then drank tea. They got the money for the tea by voluntarily contributing their own kopeks! It was quite clear of course that this music was a cover for counter-Revolutionary sentiments and that the money was being collected not for tea but to assist the dying world bourgeois. And they were all arrested and given from three to ten years – Anna Shipnikera getting five, while Ivan Nikolayevich, Varentser and the other organisers of the affair who refused to confess were shot.

From *The Gulag Archipelago,* by Alexander Solzhenitsyn

This painting called 'Higher and Higher' by S.V. Ryangina gives an optimistic and heroic image of the electrification of the USSR

The scale of the Terror

One estimate has it that up to one million people were put to death and eight million others sent to the labour camps. The murdered were often buried unceremoniously in mass graves. It is estimated that the remains of 100,000 people were buried in one mass grave alone.

With extreme irony, Stalin announced in the middle of this gruesome Terror a new Constitution in 1936. He had the audacity to call it the most democratic Constitution in the world. The truth was that the Constitution merely confirmed Stalin's dictatorial control of the USSR. He also had the history of the USSR rewritten to shower himself with praise. Opponents were downgraded and some entirely omitted from the Revolutionary years, even though they played a far more important part than Stalin.

Stalin saw to it that the influence and power of the Church was reduced. The 1936 Constitution made pro-religious propaganda a crime, although anti-religious propaganda was encouraged. The Godless League tried to convince people that religion was useless. Attacks on the Church leaders continued until, by 1939, only 4 out of the 163 bishops remained free, while only 4,000 out of 54,000 churches remained open. Thousands of mosques were also closed down. The State even tried to interfere with the Muslim pilgrimage to Mecca.

Lenin's policies towards the nationalities continued for some time. National identity was promoted through language and culture. Local language was used in official business. This meant that many languages appeared in print for the first time. But instead of this leading to the nationalities embracing Socialism, as Lenin had hoped, they sought more autonomy.

The greatest struggle of the 1930's, against the peasants who opposed collectivization, was largely a war against the national minorities (who were mostly rural). Stalin's uprooting and transporting of millions of people had a devastating effect on a number of minority groups.

▲ Two of Stalin's policies combined into one – grain confiscated from peasants in 1927 being stored in a closed down church

J Stalin encouraged the cult of the leader, and portrayed himself as a jovial, popular man. This famous photograph shows six-year-old Engelsina Chezkova meeting Stalin. A statue based upon it was erected in Moscow, called 'Thank you Comrade Stalin for my happy childhood'. In fact, Stalin had Engelsina's father shot as a spy, and her mother died young after being accused of being 'an enemy of the people'.

However, by the second half of the 1930's, a new policy was put into place reversing the earlier policy. Russification was a more forceful way of imposing a common Russian culture. Russian became compulsory in all schools and Russians were given jobs before all others, e.g army promotion went to Russians. A policy of Russification had also been adopted by the Tsar.

Stalin imprisoned or killed many of the leaders of the nationalities in the purges. Almost all of the educated Chechens were arrested. The most important leaders of the Muslim community were put through one of the show trials. In 1938 Stalin replaced the whole of the Ukrainian government with loyal Russians.

With the Party well and truly purged, and a chaotic reign of terror in the country, only the Red Army was left as a potential opponent of Stalin. He feared the army and knew that they could overthrow him. To secure his power, the army and the other forces were purged in 1937. Senior army officers were accused of spying. Even the hero of the Civil War, Marshal Tukhachevsky, the Commander-in-Chief of the Red Army, was arrested. Half of the army's officers (35,000 men) were arrested and imprisoned, even young officers fresh out of training. 13 of the 15 generals were purged. The navy was even more ruthlessly purged. When Germany invaded the USSR in 1941, the Red Army was poorly prepared. The purges had completely decapitated the armed forces. It could have led to a disaster in the war.

The purgers were themselves purged. Yagoda, the police chief who carried out the early purges, was shot in 1936 and replaced by Yezhov. After a few years Yezhov (known as the evil dwarf) was sent to a lunatic asylum and later shot. Beria, the new police chief, became the most feared man in the USSR.

By 1939 Stalin felt secure. He told the 18th Party Congress that he now had the type of intelligentsia that he wanted, i.e. those who agreed with him. The new men who had filled the dead men's shoes were technically competent and very loyal to Stalin. They were from yesterday's workers and peasants and the sons of workers and peasants, promoted to positions of command.

This is an impossible period to understand. The horror was unbelievable. The country lived in terror; conditions on the gulags were unbearably cruel; and at least one million people were killed. Why did Stalin do it? Was it the work of a madman who had lost his reason, or was he a ruthless politician intent on securing power at any cost? We know that the purges and the Terror made him the absolute ruler of the USSR. However, the cost was one of the worst crimes of the twentieth century.

1   Why was Stalin called 'an evil genius'?
2   Why do you think Stalin is suspected of involvement in the murder of Kirov?
3   Leading Communist Party officials were given carefully staged 'trials' before being executed. What was the purpose of the trials?
4   Why can't historians be certain exactly how many people died in the Purges?
5   What was the purpose of the Purges?
6   How do you think loyal Communists would have felt about the Purges?
7   How much power did Stalin have by 1940?
8   i) What was the purpose of the paintings, Sources G and I?
    ii) How can you tell?
9   i) Why did Stalin want Source J to be widely printed?
    ii) Does it have any use as an historical source?
10 With reference to the written sources, describe life in the labour camps.
11 i) How reliable are these accounts?
    ii) How did the author gather the information?

Essay:
i) What were the Purges of the 1930s?
ii) Why were they carried out and with what results?

8 *T*he road to war

Relations with other countries

When Russia became a Communist country there was outrage and fear among the Capitalist nations. They were outraged that their loans were not repaid, that religion was banned, and that Capitalism was overthrown. They also feared the Communist intention of spreading revolution worldwide, to set up similar atheistic, anti-Capitalist, Socialist states around the world. Many of the advanced Capitalist countries supported the anti-Soviet White armies in the Russian Civil War. They intervened to try to end the fledgling Communist state.

The new Soviet government was committed in the early years to the spread of Communist revolutions worldwide. The Comintern was set up in 1919 to achieve this aim. Local Communist parties, working under the close supervision of Moscow, were to prepare revolutions to overthrow Capitalism in their own countries.

But the early Communist revolutions, e.g. in Germany, were short-lived and unsuccessful. It became obvious to the new Soviet leadership that spontaneous revolutions were unlikely. An odd foreign policy then developed – theoretically the USSR supported revolution in every country, but the reality was that everyone knew that this would not happen. The Soviet government was also conscious of the West's intervention in the Civil War and their continued hostility towards the USSR. Consequently, the Soviet policy was defensive in a hostile world.

Germany was the other outcast nation. She had been blamed for the First World War and was punished severely at the Treaty of Versailles. Both outcast nations – Germany and the USSR – came together in the Treaty of Rapallo in 1922. This was the first step towards diplomatic recognition of the USSR. For Germany the Treaty helped to get around the Treaty of Versailles, which restricted their military might. They were able to re-arm with Soviet help. For the USSR there were advantages of trade but, more importantly, they felt that the Western Capitalist powers were split. Their greatest fear was a united anti-Soviet Western front. The Treaty was renewed in 1926. Stalin was pleased with the supply of German know how – modern factories, especially armament factories, were built with German technical expertize in the Soviet Union.

The Treaty of Locarno in 1925 was deeply worrying for the USSR. In it the western borders of Germany, which had been set down in the Treaty of Versailles, were ratified. However, nothing was said about Germany's eastern borders. Would Germany be allowed to revise her eastern borders in the future? An expanding Germany going east would clearly be a threat to the USSR.

Yet in the same year, 1925, a number of countries had begun to recognise the USSR. She was recognised by Britain, Germany, France, Italy, and Japan. Stalin's policy of 'Socialism in one country' was much less threatening than Trotsky's call for world revolution. Stalin remained nominally in favour of exporting revolution, but his real intention was to protect the interests of the USSR.

In 1928 the USSR joined with other countries in 'outlawing war as an instrument of foreign policy'. This optimistic Kellogg-Briand Pact showed that the USSR was taking its place among the nations of the earth. Others were cautiously relieved to see her renounce war. Even the USA recognised the USSR in 1933. America remained apprehensive though. America feared the potential of the

There are two kinds of war and where there are two kinds of war there are two kinds of peace. There are international and civil wars, and of these the civil is more horrible. It is a fair question to ask whether the Soviet government has set its face against civil as resolutely as against international war. For years past the whole basis of Soviet world policy has been to produce armed insurrection, amounting to civil war, in every country where they can exert influence. We ought to be told whether the Soviets have decided no longer to interfere in the affairs of other nations.

Lord Cushendun here expressed what many felt about the Soviet policy of supporting revolutions abroad, which questioned their commitment to renouncing war as an instrument of foreign policy.

USSR and, like many others, opposed her anti-religious, anti-Capitalist politics. The USSR was finally admitted to the League of Nations in 1934, which showed fairly widespread acceptance of the Soviet Union. However, Hitler came to power in Germany in 1933. His foreign policy was to change European and world politics.

The USSR was directly affected by Hitler's coming to power. Stalin's policy of controlling local Communist parties had backfired in 1933. He had instructed the German Communist Party (KPD) not to join with the other left wing parties. The failure of the KPD and the Socialist Party (SPD) to join in alliance against Hitler unwittingly allowed Hitler to come to power. Hitler's policy was to expand Germany a) by regaining territory lost at the Treaty of Versailles and b) by extending eastwards into Russia. According to Hitler, the Germans were a master race, greater than supposedly lesser peoples like the Jews and the Slavs – the Russians were Slavs. Germany, according to Hitler, needed living space (lebensraum). This increased living space was to be in Russia. Understandably, Stalin was fearful of this policy of lebensraum.

B

We turn our eyes to the east. This huge empire in the east is ripe for ending. The future aim of our foreign policy ought to be to acquire such eastern territory as is needed for our German people. Only a large space on this earth assures a nation of freedom. The National Socialist movement must hold to its aim to secure for the German people the land and soil to which they are entitled. If we speak of soil in Europe today we can have in mind only Russia and her border states.

From *Mein Kampf,* by Adolf Hitler. Here we see quite clearly what Hitler's intentions were.

Reactions to Hitler

Soviet foreign policy changed quickly in recognition of the changed circumstances. They became firm supporters in the League of Nations of collective security. In fact, they became increasingly critical of the League's policy of appeasement towards Hitler. Stalin also instructed the Communist parties abroad to change their tactics. They were from now on to join with other left wing parties in a broad popular front coalition against Fascism. When the civil war broke out in Spain in 1936 between the Nationalist right wing (supported by the Fascist governments in Germany and Italy) and the Republican left wing forces, Stalin supported the left wing

Popular Front. However, he feared direct confrontation and open war with Germany, so he was not willing to give too much support to the Republicans. He was concerned that if he sent very large forces to secure a left wing government in power, the other Western powers might join in an anti-Soviet war. Spain was also very far away from the USSR. Stalin did not want independent Socialist states, instead he wanted satellite states directly under his control. The key issues for Stalin were Soviet security and direct control by Stalin. To secure both of these aims he sent only enough supplies to keep the war going, hoping, thereby, to distract the Fascists' attention away from him.

Munich and after

By 1938 Hitler had challenged the Treaty of Versailles and got his own way. He had audaciously moved his troops into the Rhineland in 1936 and joined Austria and Germany together in 1938. His next target was the Sudetenland in Czechoslovakia, which contained a large German population. He was demanding that the Sudetenland be handed over to Germany. The Western powers, anxious to appease Hitler and to avoid war at any cost, agreed at a conference in Munich in 1938 that the Sudetenland could be annexed by Hitler. Britain, France, Germany, and Italy agreed that Czechoslovakia should give up this territory (no Czechs were at this meeting). Stalin was not invited to the conference. This was odd as he could have played a valuable part.

The West were seemingly willing to overlook the defence treaty which the USSR had with Czechoslovakia. In this treaty, they agreed to defend Czechoslovakia if France would also. Stalin suspected the West's intentions. It seemed to him that the West was allowing, even encouraging, Hitler to move eastwards. They knew that the German policy was to build an empire in the east at the expense of the USSR.

'What, no chair for me?' by David Low, published in September 1938

Was the West behaving at Munich in 1938 as it had done at Locarno in 1925, i.e. to encourage German expansion towards the east? Suspecting that the West had this attitude; clearly aware that his purged military forces were poorly prepared for war; and with Germany's intention to expand into the USSR well known, Stalin needed time and allies to prepare for the inevitable war.

'On the Great European Road', by Boris Efimov. The Russian abbreviation for USSR is CCCP.

As Germany was posing a threat to the peace of Europe, it was natural that the other European powers would begin negotiations to form an alliance against Hitler. Britain, France, and the USSR did begin talks. They could have formed a very effective alliance against Hitler. However, the distrust of Stalin by the British and the French was too great. The feeling in both countries was that Stalin was worse than Hitler. The purges, they felt, confirmed this.

The British Prime Minister, Neville Chamberlain, openly confessed that he distrusted the USSR. To him their motives were suspect. He felt that he had little in common with them because they were a totalitarian state. He also said that they were not likely to be a very effective fighting force. Winston Churchill, who was the most outspoken opponent of Hitler in Britain, disagreed with Chamberlain. He believed that an alliance should have been formed between Britain, France, and the USSR, which would have alarmed the Germans and maybe even have prevented war. When Stalin failed to form an alliance with Britain and France, he began to look elsewhere.

A German cartoon about the failure of the British and French to ally with the USSR against Germany in Spring 1939

F

France and Britain don't want to get involved in a war with Hitler. They are still hoping to push Hitler into a war with the Soviet Union. By refusing to make an agreement with us, they tried to allow Hitler to attack the Soviet Union. They will have to pay the price for their short-sighted policy.

Stalin summing up how he felt about Britain and France

The Nazi-Soviet Pact

In May 1939, Molotov became the Soviet Minister for Foreign Affairs. His instructions were to negotiate an alliance with Germany! This Nazi-Soviet Pact was signed in August 1939. In the Pact they both agreed not to go to war with each other. Poland was to be divided between them. The USSR was to have control of eastern Poland, Latvia, Estonia, Lithuania, Finland, and parts of Romania. This was an extraordinary treaty: it changed the map of Eastern Europe; it gave the USSR vast extra territory; and it turned the foreign policies of both countries upside down. Germany was violently anti-Communist, while the USSR was equally hostile to Fascism. Communists and diplomats were confused the world over. According to one British M.P., 'it was the doubled-dyed treachery of the Kremlin'.

The signing of the Nazi-Soviet Pact in Moscow in August 1939

'Rendevous' by David Low, published on 20th September 1939. Hitler and Stalin are meeting over the body of Poland. Hitler had invaded on 1st September and Stalin on 17th September. This was the result of a secret agreement in the Nazi-Soviet Pact to divide Poland between them.

H

Britain, France, and the USA, by rejecting the idea of collective security proposed by the USSR, played into the hands of the aggressors (Germany). The great powers (Britain, France, and the USA) wanted to direct the German Fascist aggression eastwards, against the USSR. The disgraceful Munich deal (where Britain and France allowed Germany to take the Sudetenland from Czechoslovakia), and the Anglo-German and Franco-German treaties of non-aggression which followed, helped Germany to turn her aggression towards the USSR. The Munich policy of appeasement pushed Europe to the brink of war.

At the same time the Soviet Union tried to make peace. In March 1939 the Soviet Union opened talks with Britain and France to discuss ways of preventing Fascist aggression. These talks, which lasted until August 1939, showed how unwilling Britain and France were to set up collective security against Hitler. As a result, the Soviet Union stood alone in the face of the growing Fascist menace. In this situation the USSR took the only correct decision: when she was asked by Germany to make a treaty of non-aggression, the Soviet Union agreed. The Russo-German Non-Aggression Pact was signed in August 1939. The Soviet Union agreed to the Pact with Germany only when it became clear that Britain and France were totally unwilling to stand up to the Fascist aggressors with the USSR.

Some Western historians tried to prove in vain that the Pact helped to start the Second World War. The truth is that it helped to stop the united front against the USSR and it gave the USSR precious time in which to strengthen its defences. The Soviet Union was clearly aware that Germany would at some time attack the USSR.

Adapted from *A History of the USSR,* by Kukushkin, 1981. This illustrates the official Soviet view of this period.

Ready for war

Stalin had bought the time he needed to build up his forces in preparation for war. He had won extensive territory, all of which would be used as a buffer, he hoped, against the likely German invasion. Later these areas were to be secured for the USSR by the NKVD. The policy was called pacification. What they did was to deport any potential opposition. In true NKVD form they drew up long lists of all likely opponents. Some of the lists even included members of stamp collecting clubs! The hated Treaty of Brest-Litovsk, where Russia had lost so much territory, was overthrown. The old borders of Tsarist Russia were to be restored. Germany, for its part, did not have to fear a repeat of the First World War with a war on two fronts. The Soviet Union also agreed to supply Germany with food, fuel, and raw materials for their arms industry. Some of these supplies were en route to Germany on the night of 22nd June 1941 when Germany, as expected, broke the Nazi-Soviet Pact and invaded the Soviet Union.

1   Why was the Comintern set up?
2   i) What were Lord Cushendun's concerns in Source A?
    ii) Why did Britain, France, and the USA distrust the USSR?
3   With reference to Source B, explain Stalin's fears when Hitler took power in Germany.
4   In Source C which countries' leaders are shown sitting down?
5   Did it matter that the USSR was left out of the Munich Conference?
6   In Source G explain why Stalin and Hitler are shown insulting each other and at the same time bowing to each other.

7   i) What reasons are given in Source H for the Russo-German Pact?
    ii) How reliable is the Source?
8   i) How do Sources C, D, E and G support Source H?
    ii) How useful are cartoons as historical evidence?
9   Was it partly the fault of Britain and France that the USSR made the Pact with Germany?
10 How did the USSR try to protect herself against Nazi aggression?

Essay: 'Stalin had no choice but to make a pact with Nazi Germany in 1939.' Do you agree with this opinion?

9 The Great Patriotic War

Germany Invades

The German army invaded the Soviet Union on 22nd June 1941. As expected, Hitler tore up the Nazi-Soviet Non-Aggression Pact, which was no more than a marriage of convenience for both sides. Hitler hated Communism and had always planned extra living space for the Germans by using Russian land. He also wanted to use the resources of the rich oil fields of the Caucasus and the fertile lands of the Ukraine to supply Germany. He had told his generals: 'the sooner we smash Russia the better.' Hitler claimed that this operation, code named Barbarossa, was the greatest military campaign ever launched. It was an awesome display of German military might: 160 divisions advancing along a 3,000 mile front.

Stalin, it appears, was caught unawares. He had not expected the Nazi-Soviet Pact to be broken, at least not then. He had received plenty of advanced warning of the planned attack from his own sources in Japan and in Britain. However, he believed right up until the last minute that it would be possible to ward off an attack through diplomacy. Soviet forces on the frontline only received warning of a possible attack on the evening of 21st June.

Stalin had failed to make the necessary preparations for war. The leadership of the army was found to be sadly wanting. The new generals, who had replaced those who were purged, were often not up to the job. The Soviet forces were short of supplies and the Soviet people, who had been bombarded with propaganda about the friendship with Germany, were unprepared for war.

The German lightning attack (Blitzkrieg) caught the Soviets unawares. The Luftwaffe destroyed much of the Soviet air force while it was still on the ground. With control of the air the German army advanced rapidly into Soviet territory. The Germans began to lay siege to Leningrad on 8th September. By the Autumn they had taken Kiev, the capital of the Ukraine, and by December they were outside Moscow. They captured hundreds of thousands of Soviet soldiers. The SS took over captured civilians and murdered many of them.

This Soviet poster graphically shows atrocities carried out by German SS soldiers during their advance through the Soviet Union

Reaction and resistance

There is some controversy surrounding Stalin's role in the early days of the German attack. Little is known about his actions for about two weeks. According to some observers he suffered a nervous breakdown, others say that he was deeply depressed. Whatever the truth of those first few weeks, he emerged to address the nation. He appealed to their nationalism, their love of country, to their patriotism. Nothing was said of defending Socialism or Communism. This was to be a nationalistic campaign to save mother Russia; a patriotic war was to be fought, led by the patriotic leader Stalin.

A

> Comrades, citizens, brothers and sisters, fighters of our army and navy. I am speaking to you my friends.
>
> The enemy is cruel. He is out to seize our lands … our grain and oil. He is out to restore the rule of the landlords, to turn our peoples into the slaves of German Princes. In case of a forced retreat the enemy must not be left a single engine, a single pound of grain or a gallon of fuel. All valuable property, including grain and fuel, that cannot be withdrawn must be destroyed without fail. In areas occupied by the enemy, guerrillas must be formed, sabotage groups must be organised to combat the enemy … to blow up bridges and roads.

From Stalin's broadcast to the nation on 3rd July 1941. When he heard this broadcast one of the generals said 'we suddenly seemed to feel much stronger'.

Stalin needed an ally during the war and turned to the Church. The Church blessed the work of 'our government' and condemned traitors among the clergy and laity who made the Germans welcome. Any traitors were to be excommunicated (expelled from the Church). The Church was restored to its former role. Stalin hoped that services of thanksgiving during successful battles would inspire patriotism.

Moscow women digging an anti-tank ditch to defend the city against the advancing German army in 1941

In 1943 he allowed the Orthodox Church to elect a new leader (Patriarch). Some theological colleges were allowed to reopen. By 1945, 24,000 churches were reopened and 74 bishops were back in office. It suited Stalin to use the Church as a unifying force in the country. Stalin was very anxious to avoid a situation where the Church might encourage anti-Soviet activity during the war.

A thanksgiving church service being held in Moscow, after the Germans had been pushed back from the city

All differences between Church and State were forgotten during the war: anti-religious propaganda died away and the rules about teaching children their religion were relaxed. We can see this reconciliation in the words of the leader of the Moslem community: 'May Allah help you to bring to a victorious end your work of freeing the oppressed peoples. Amen'.

Even though the German army captured hundreds of miles of Soviet territory, they had overlooked the size of the USSR – it covered one sixth of the land surface of the earth. Stalin knew that the German army would need to live off the land as they could not successfully supply their armies from Germany. Consequently, he ordered a scorched earth policy which was intended to leave the Germans with very little. As the Soviets withdrew, they blew up bridges and dams and they burned crops. Stalin was even willing to forsake some of the most prestigious showpieces of the Five Year Plans. Tallin, the capital of Estonia, was left in flames as the population was evacuated.

Stalingrad

While the siege of Leningrad was bogged down, the Germans launched another offensive. They wanted to take the rich oil fields of the Caucasus. Hitler also ordered that the city of Stalingrad be taken. Even though it wasn't stategically significant, it was critical in Hitler's eyes because it bore Stalin's name. It became a symbol to both sides. A large German army of 300,000 men laid siege to Stalingrad.

The city had been turned into something which none of those who fought there had ever imagined and none who survived could ever forget.

The closest and bloodiest battle of the war was fought among the stumps of buildings burnt or burning. From afar, Stalingrad looked like a furnace, yet inside men froze. Dogs rushed into the Volga to drown rather than endure any longer the perils of the shore. The no less desperate men were reduced to automatons obeying orders until it came to their turn to die, human only in their suffering.

From *Total War,* by Calvocoressi and Wint, 1972

Soviet troops attacking German positions in the frozen ruins of the Red October Factory in Stalingrad

The fighting was intense with the Soviets fighting to hold every street and every building. Even individual rooms were contested.

While this hand to hand fighting went on in the city, the Germans were themselves encircled by Marshall Zhukov. Soon Von Paulus, the commander of the German 6th Army, realised that the position was hopeless. He asked for permission to surrender to save the lives of his starving and freezing men. Hitler refused: 'Surrender is forbidden. The army will hold their positions to the last man and the last round of ammunition.' Von Paulus was forced to continue his hopeless position. His army were attacked for another two months through a relentless winter. He finally surrendered in February 1943. By then, he was reduced to only 90,000 men. With over 200,000 German soldiers dead and 90,000 taken prisoner, it was seen as a momentous victory. Stalingrad showed that Germany could be beaten. It was a turning point in the Soviet campaign, indeed one of the decisive battles of the war itself. Throughout the war we see the scale of Russian suffering and casualties. They lost more men in the Battle of Stalingrad than the Americans lost in the whole of the war.

The other key battle of 1943 was the Battle of Kursk. This was Hitler's last great offensive against the Soviet Union. He used his latest tanks and newest guns. Over one million men and 3,000 tanks were involved in this set piece. The German Panthers and Tigers were defeated by the Russians. Hitler lost another army with some of his best modern equipment and most experienced men. The victory at Kursk was a tribute not only to the Russian tank commanders but also to the success of the Five Year Plans and the decision to build factories in the east, far out of the Germans' range. From now on the Russian army was on the offensive.

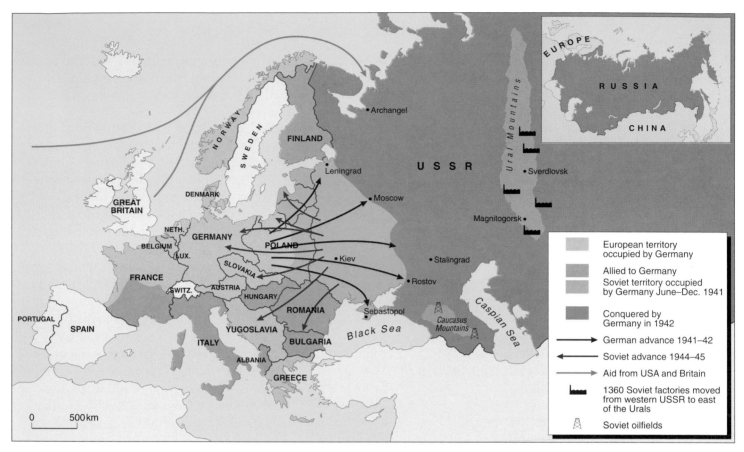

Leningrad

The siege of Leningrad dragged on and on. Hitler wanted the city where Communism had started to be taken and razed to the ground.

▼ C

The Fuhrer has decided to raze the city of Leningrad from the face of the earth. It is proposed to blockade the city closely … with artillery and with ceaseless bombardment from the air. If this creates a situation in the city which produces calls for surrender they will be refused.

From a German army directive about Leningrad

The siege lasted for 900 days. The Soviets kept some supplies coming through across the frozen Lake Ladoga. However, food became so scarce that people began to eat their own pets. The citizens suffered from cold, disease, and constant bombardment from the Germans. The siege is described by the poet Mikhail Dudin: 'Ice bound trams and trolley buses, broken and grotesquely tangled wires hanging from above – in the dusk hours figures would pass here and there, pulling a hand made sledge loaded with something swathed like a mummy. This is how people who died from starvation made their last journey.' When the siege was lifted by the arrival of another Russian army, 800,000 Russians had died.

▲

The Eastern Front in the Second World War. The inset map shows the total size of the Soviet Union compared to the battle zone.

▼ D

1941
 December 28th – Zhenya died at 12.30 in the morning.
1942
 January 25th – Babushka died at 3 o' clock.
 March 17th – Leka died at 5 o' clock in the morning
 April 13th – Dedya Vasya died at 2 o' clock at night
 May 10th – Dedya Lisha died at 4 o' clock in the afternoon.
 May 13th – Mama died at 7.30 am
 Svichevs died. All died. Only Tanya remains.

These entries from the diary of Tanya Savicheva, a young Leningrad girl, tell the tragic story of her family

 A child's body swathed in cloth is dragged away for burial on a sledge during the siege of Leningrad

Victory at great cost

In 1944 the Red Army went on the offensive. They pushed westwards. By early 1945 they were in Poland, Hungary, Romania, and Yugoslavia. All the territory taken by the Germans was retaken by 1945. By May 1945, Berlin had fallen to the Red Army, thus ending the war in Europe.

 Soviet soldiers fly the red flag from the roof of the Reichstag in the centre of Berlin in May 1945

F

The repressive censorship of the 1930's was lifted during the war and writers went to the front to describe the war in detail. Many novels appeared which praised the heroic Soviet generals, maybe to help the ordinary soldier to overcome a lack of trust in the high command. The sieges of Leningrad and Stalingrad produced strong emotional literature praising the heroism of the ordinary citizens.

E

You
    The Living
        Know
            That from this land
                We did not mean to go

We made our stand
    By the Neva

We did not fear to give
    Freely of our lives
        That you might live

An epitaph to the citizens of Leningrad, written by Robert Rozhdestvensky, summing up their heroism

The Russo-German campaigns were the most terrible war that has ever been waged. The numbers of dead were huge.
If the weather was fine men might go through the motions of ordinary life and, with their singing and horseplay, behave as though they were on an excursion rather than a highly organised killing. But then for many months there would be slush and mud and clothes never really dry, or the intense cold which made it dangerous to take off a glove.
    The most remarkable thing about this war was that on both sides men went on fighting it for nearly four years.

From *Total War* by Calvocoressi and Wint, 1972

Among some non-Russians there had been sympathy for the Germans. The Lithuanians had staged an anti-Russian

rebellion and the Ukrainian anti-Soviet partisans had killed Red Army General Vatutin. An anti-Soviet army was also formed under General Vlasov which fought for the Germans. The Vlasovite army was handed back to the USSR in 1945 by the allies; Vlasov was hanged in Red Square on a meat hook. Stalin was swift and brutal in his response to any national dissent during the war. Anyone accused of collaboration with the Germans was deported; often people were deported simply on the suspicion of what the secret police thought they might be capable of. The Volga Germans and Crimean Tartars were transported to the east in unspeakable conditions with many dying en route. The victims were sometimes just left in the open countryside and left to try to survive. The Lithuanian deportation figures tell their own grim story: 100,000 deported in 1946, 70,000 in 1947, 70,000 in 1948, and 40,000 in 1949.

It was time to count the cost of the war. Twenty million Soviet citizens had died. More than one in ten of the population had died in the four years of Russian involvement. In fact, the Soviet Union lost more people than all the other allies put together. Cities were ruined, animals

killed. In some villages so many men and horses had been killed that women were harnessed to pull the ploughs after the war. Many of the five million Russian prisoners of war who were released from German captivity were sent straight into Soviet labour camps – such was Stalin's suspicion of his own people. Others, like Solzhenitsyn, were sent to the labour camps accused by the NKVD of criticizing Stalin.

Soviet refugees returning to their town after the battle has moved on. The wooden buildings have all burnt to the ground and only the brick chimneys remain standing.

Survivers searching for their loved ones among the dead, after a German massacre of civilians at the town of Kerch in the Crimea

The wartime alliance

The wartime alliance with Britain and America had always been tense. They were bound together by a common enemy and no more. Stalin was suspicious of their motives (especially of Britain's) and they of his. He had argued that he was shouldering an unfair load in the war. Germany had committed two thirds of her army in Russia. Stalin wanted Britain and America to open up a second front against Germany to relieve the pressure on the Soviet Union. He was very critical of their delay in doing this. Britain was suspicious of Stalin's intentions once the war was over. Officially the governments emphasised their friendship towards each other. The Americans sent large quantities of essential resources to the Soviet Union. There was plenty of propaganda in Britain which praised 'our gallant Russian ally'. Stalin, for his part, dissolved the Comintern (which promoted Communist revolution abroad) in 1943.

Stalin wanted a post-war settlement which guaranteed the security of the Soviet Union. He achieved this at the wartime conferences which decided strategy and planned the political make up of post-war Europe. At Teheran in 1943, it was agreed that Russia was to move into the Balkans to liberate that area from the Germans. It was also agreed that Russia could keep control of Estonia, Latvia, and Lithuania. The allies also agreed at the Moscow Conference in 1944 to spheres of influence in Europe. Stalin's sphere of influence was to be Eastern Europe. He agreed at Yalta in February 1945 to hold free elections in the areas of Eastern Europe under his control. Yalta also allowed him to hold onto the Polish territory which he had taken in 1939. These agreements secured Soviet security. However, they were to lead to tensions after the war was over. These tensions became part of the Cold War.

British Prime Minister Churchill, and US President Roosevelt, with Stalin at the Yalta Conference in February 1945

1 What factors made the German attack on the USSR so successful?
2 What possible explanations could there be for the two week delay before Stalin's broadcast in Source A?
3 How do you think Russians would have felt when they heard the broadcast?
4 What did Stalin order the people to do in Source A?
5 Explain the reasons for Stalin's change of policy towards the Churches.
6 How do you think people would have felt when they heard reports from Leningrad during the siege?
7 How significant was the German defeat at Stalingrad?

8 With reference to the map of the Eastern Front, explain some of the difficulties which Hitler faced.
9 Why do you think that for many years after the war the Russians felt hatred towards the Germans?
10 What effect do you think the war had on the Russian people's opinion of Stalin?
11 i) Why were there tensions between the USSR and their allies, Britain and the USA?
ii) Could events before the war have played any part?

Essay: 'Hitler's fatal mistake was to invade the USSR.' Explain the truth of this statement.

10 *Cold War*

The wartime alliance between the Soviet Union and her allies was often tense. When the war was over and the alliance came to an end, relations between the Soviet Union and America became hostile. Hostile relations soon deteriorated into what was called the Cold War. This was not a war in the conventional sense, where armies fight each other, rather it was a war of words, a test of nerve – going to the point of war, without actually fighting. Neither side could afford to start a conventional war because of the destructive horror of nuclear weapons.

Strains in the alliance

There had been strains in the alliance during the war. The USA and the USSR were strange bedfellows. They were united only in their opposition to Hitler and Fascism. Churchill explained the need for an alliance with the Communists like this: 'If Hitler invaded hell I would make at least a favourable reference to the devil'.

The Soviet Union distrusted the West. Russia had been invaded by Germany in 1914, and the West had joined the White armies in the Russian Civil War to put down the Communists. Germany had invaded Russia again in 1941, after Britain and France had refused to make an alliance with Russia against Germany in March 1939. The Soviets felt that they had good reason to be suspicious. Stalin's suspicions of America deepened when America developed the atomic bomb. America kept the development a secret and refused to share the technological know-how with the Soviets. The American President, Truman, boasted that with the atom bomb: 'We would have the hammer on those boys'. The American Secretary of State (Foreign Minister) Byrne revealed the superior attitude which the bomb gave America: 'The bomb might well put us in a position to dictate our own terms.' Relations deteriorated when the Americans dropped the atomic bombs on Japan. This last military act of the Second World War was the first diplomatic act of the Cold War. It clearly told the Soviet Union that she had no part to play in the future of Japan; and to take note of American superior military technology.

Whilst America's strength lay in the atomic bomb, Stalin relied on his awesomely large armies, which, unlike the American army, had not demobilised after the war. Churchill expressed the West's fear for the future of Europe because of the huge Soviet army stationed in Eastern Europe: 'What will be the position in a year or two when the British and American armies have faded and Russia may choose to keep two or three hundred divisions on active service?'

Eastern Europe

The Soviet Union's take-over of Eastern Europe was at the heart of the West's fears and suspicions. During the war-time conference at Casablanca, it had been agreed that the Soviet Union should liberate Eastern Europe from Germany. Churchill had also agreed post-war spheres of influence with Stalin in Moscow in 1944. Churchill himself describes the meeting.

I said 'Let us settle our affairs in the Balkans. Your armies are in Romania and Bulgaria. So far as Britain and Russia are concerned, how would it do for you to have 90% predominance (control) in Romania, for us to have 90% of the say in Greece, and then go 50\50 in Yugoslavia?'

I then wrote out the percentage figures on a half sheet of paper, adding Hungary 50\50, Bulgaria 75\25 (to Soviet advantage).

I pushed this across to Stalin ... there was a slight pause. Then he took his blue pencil and made a large tick upon it. At length I said 'Might it not be thought rather cynical if it seemed we had disposed of these issues so fateful to millions of people, in such an offhand manner? Let us burn the paper.'

'No, you keep it' said Stalin.

From *The Second World War* by Winston Churchill

Churchill returned from that meeting saying: 'Poland should be allowed to have the government in any way her people choose ... provided it is not on Fascist lines and provided Poland stands loyally as a friend of Russia.' He was acknowledging that, for security reasons (remember that the Soviet Union had been twice invaded through Poland in the twentieth century), the Soviet Union wanted control over the countries on her border.

At the Yalta Conference in February 1945, when most of Eastern Europe had been liberated by the Soviet army, Stalin promised to hold free elections in the occupied territories. He also agreed to allow other parties as well as the Communist parties to share in the government. It soon became obvious that he had no intention of fulfilling that promise. Maybe it was naive of the West to expect such a dictator with his track record for undemocratic rule to agree to free elections. His intention was to create a buffer zone of Communist-controlled states. The only way that America could insist on free elections was by going to war. This she was reluctant to do. Not only was she exhausted after the Second World War, but she had also demobilised her military forces and the only way to win such a war was by using nuclear weapons. Churchill described the take-over of Eastern Europe to his American audience in Fulton, Missouri as an Iron Curtain descending on Europe.

Winston Churchill making his famous speech at Fulton, Missouri in March 1946

B

From Stettin in the Baltic to Trieste on the Adriatic, an Iron Curtain has descended across the continent. Behind that line lie all the capitals of the ancient states of Central and Eastern Europe. Warsaw, Berlin, Prague, Vienna, Budapest, Belgrade, Bucharest, and Sofia, all those famous cities and the populations around them lie in the Soviet sphere and are all subject, in one way or another, to a very high and increasing measure of control from Moscow. In other countries, Communist parties or fifth columns constitute a growing challenge and peril to Christian civilisation.

From what I have seen of our Russian friends and allies during the war, I am convinced that there is nothing they admire so much as strength, and there is nothing for which they have less respect than for military weakness. If the Western democracies stand together in strict adherence (loyalty) to the principles of the United Nations charter ... if they become divided catastrophe may overwhelm us all.

From Churchill's speech at Fulton, Missouri, 1946

Mr Churchill now takes the stand of the warmongers and he is not alone. He has friends not only in Britain but in the United States.

The following circumstances should not be forgotten. The Germans made their invasion of the USSR through Finland, Poland, Romania, Bulgaria, and Hungary ... Governments hostile to the Soviet Union existed in those countries. As a result of the German invasion the Soviet Union has lost irretrievably in the fighting against the Germans. In other words the Soviet Union's loss of life has been several times greater than that of Britain and the United States put together. And so what can be surprising about the fact that the Soviet Union, anxious for its future safety, is trying to see to it that governments loyal to the Soviet Union should exist in these countries? How can anyone who has not taken leave of his senses describe these peaceful hopes of the Soviet Union as expansionist?

Churchill's criticism and his rallying cry for the West to oppose the Soviet Union brought this swift defensive response from Stalin, suggesting that the West did not understand his reasons

Stalin's reply explains his fears – even though the Soviet Union was one of the victors of the war, 20 million Soviet citizens had been killed. Stalin was determined that the Soviet Union would never again be vulnerable to invasion. Control of Eastern Europe would ensure a buffer zone against invasion.

Throughout occupied Eastern Europe the Communist Party controlled the coalition governments (a number of political parties held power) until the promised elections were held. They were neither free nor fair. The elections were rigged: ballot boxes went missing; opposition candidates were bullied into not standing for election; families of leading non-Communist politicians were threatened; some disappeared; Jan Masaryk, the Czech Foreign Minister, fell to his death in mysterious circumstances in 1948. Thus the Communist Party took power in Eastern Europe. Soon local European Communists were replaced with pro-Stalin Communists. Yugoslavia was the exception to this total Stalinist control of the Eastern Bloc. Marshal Tito had led the Yugoslav resistance against the Germans without the help of the Red Army. Tito's Yugoslavia, although Communist, was independent of Stalin – much to Stalin's annoyance. The Eastern Bloc countries were Stalin's puppets. They received their orders through Cominform, which ensured that they knew what Stalin wanted of them and they obeyed completely.

The Communist take-over of Eastern Europe, 1945–1949

Containment

America's greatest fear was that Communism would spread throughout the rest of Europe; countries would fall to Communism like dominoes. So they decided to contain Communism within its present borders.

The Greek Communists were fighting the royalist government for control of Greece in a bloody civil war. America feared that Greece might fall to Communism. Britain, who had supported the Greek royalists, announced that she could no longer afford to continue the support. Truman, the American President, decided to help the Greek government to oppose the Communists. In 1947 he announced his new policy.

I believe it must be the policy of the United States to support free peoples who are resisting attempted subjugation (control) by armed minorities or by outside pressure. I believe that we must assist free peoples to work out their own destinies in their own way. I believe that our help should be primarily through economic and financial aid.

From the Truman Doctrine, 1947

America was committing itself to a crusade against Communism. It meant that America would support any country anywhere that was resisting the Communists. Initially this was to be through financial help. To the Soviets this was further evidence of American aggression against them. They argued that they weren't involved in Greece. They were not.

E

The next step along the road of worsening relations with the USSR was the Truman Doctrine, which meant in reality the rearming of Greece and Turkey and the building of bases in these countries for American strategic bombers. These actions were screened, of course, by pompous pronouncements about defending democracy and peace.

A Russian historian's view of the Truman Doctrine, 1948

The Marshall Plan

At the same time, the American Secretary of State, George Marshall, announced his Plan to give billions of dollars in aid to Europe. He claimed that it was not directed against any country or doctrine, but against hunger, poverty, desperation, and chaos. Churchill called it a most unselfish act.

F

This Punch cartoon by E.H. Shepard, 'Neighbours "Come on, Sam! It's up to us again"', was published on 1st October 1947. It shows George Marshall using American aid to prop up Western Europe, which is in danger of collapse.

The Americans believed that a healthy European economy was unlikely to become Communist, whereas if the people were hungry they might see Communism as a solution. The Plan, therefore, was an attempt to kill Communism with kindness. According to Marshall: 'Without the Marshall Plan it would have been difficult for Western Europe to remain free from the tyranny of Communism. Moscow soon realised that when the Marshall Plan began to function the opportunity to Communise Western Europe would be lost.

G

The United States should do whatever it is able to do to assist in the return of normal economic health in the world, without which there can be no political stability and no assured peace. Our policy is directed not against any country or doctrine, but against hunger, poverty, desperation and chaos. Its purpose should be the revival of a working economy in the world so as to permit the emergence of political and social conditions in which free institutions can exist.

From George Marshall's speech introducing the Marshall Plan, 1947

The Soviet reaction

The money was offered to all European countries, both East and West. A number of Eastern European countries, like Czechoslovakia, were anxious to join, hoping that the money would help to rebuild their countries. The Soviet Union refused to let them, calling it 'dollar imperialism'. They argued that it would give the Americans far too much influence in Europe. Stalin feared that the Eastern Bloc countries might be coaxed away from his sphere of influence. Therefore, none of the Eastern Bloc countries were allowed to accept the Plan. The Soviet attitude is explained in Source H.

H

Thus the Marshall Plan widely advertised as a plan to 'save peace' was essentially aimed at uniting bourgeois countries on an anti-Soviet basis. Even right wing politicians and publicists (supporters in the press) saw the Marshall Plan as the nucleus (beginning) of a new Holy Alliance against Communism.

A Soviet historian's view of the Marshall Plan

I

President Truman has announced the following principles of American foreign policy. The United States will everywhere support, with weapons and money, reactionaries, Fascists who are hateful to their own people but who, on the other hand, are ready to place their country under American control. Two countries suitable for this were found at once: Greece and Turkey. Now they both have in fact come under American domination. Americans are building their military bases there, American capitalists are opening businesses and buying up all that seems to them profitable. For this the Greek and Turkish reactionaries who are in power are receiving from the Americans money and weapons for the struggle against their own people. But Greece and Turkey are too small, and American appetites are great. American expansionists are dreaming of all Europe, or at least Western Europe.
Directly to propose that the European countries become American colonies such as Greece and Turkey is somewhat inconvenient. And so the Marshall Plan emerges in America. It was announced that the United States wanted to 'help' the European countries to reconstruct their war-torn economies. Many believed this. But it was soon evident that the Marshall Plan was simply a cunning way of subjecting all Europe to American capital.

This extract from a Communist youth newspaper argues that the Marshall Plan was not an attempt to reconstruct the war-torn economies of Europe. It was simply a cunning way of subjecting all Europe to American capital.

The Truman Doctrine and the Marshall Plan showed that Europe was divided into two camps – one Soviet dominated, and the other supported by America. Relations between the two superpowers worsened when the Soviets supported the Czech Communists in assuming power in a coup in 1948. Things got worse over Berlin in the same year.

Germany

Germany's future was the focus of superpower rivalry from 1945 onwards. It was decided at Yalta in February 1945 to divide Germany into four zones, occupied by the allied powers. Britain, France, and the USA were to control the Western parts of Germany, while the Soviet Union controlled East Germany. Berlin lay in the Soviet Sector in the East, but because of its significance (like London to Britain) it too was divided among the four powers.

Relations between the four powers in the Allied Control Commission was never very good. Things got tense as the Cold War got worse. By 1948 the Western countries and the Soviets were barely on speaking terms. When the Western countries decided to reform the German currency, the Soviets saw this as an attempt to control the economy of all Germany. Berlin was a constant source of embarrassment to Stalin. Western propaganda in the media and the standard of living there was too much for him. He decided to force the other powers out of Berlin. In June 1948 the Soviet army cut off the road and rail links between West Berlin and the Western Sector of Germany. Stalin had hoped that the West would give in. Any attempt to force the road and rail links open could have led to war, possibly a nuclear war. America was aware of the danger but was reluctant to give in. They thought that if Berlin fell, the rest of Germany would fall next and so on in a domino fashion. So they decided to feed Berlin and its 2 million people by air. For ten months America and Britain supplied Berlin this way. They knew that Stalin would not risk starting a war by shooting down one of the supply planes.

The division of Germany and Berlin after the Second World War

▼

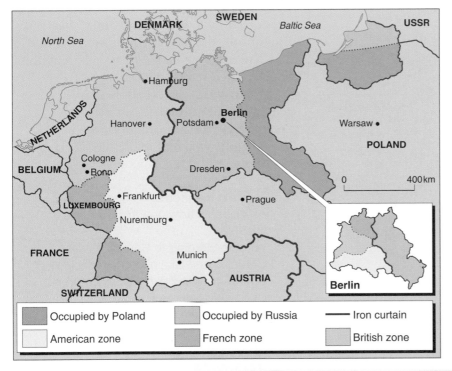

Occupied by Poland	Occupied by Russia	Iron curtain
American zone	French zone	British zone

▶

Berliners queueing up for food during the Berlin blockade, 1948

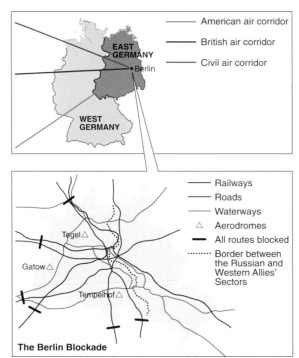

American aircraft unloading cargoes of food at Tempelhof Airport in Berlin during the Soviet blockade in 1948

This map shows the blockade of West Berlin by the Soviet Union

EAST GERMANY
Berlin
WEST GERMANY

——— American air corridor
——— British air corridor
——— Civil air corridor

——— Railways
——— Roads
——— Waterways
△ Aerodromes
▬ All routes blocked
······ Border between the Russian and Western Allies' Sectors

Tegel △
Gatow △
Tempelhof △

The Berlin Blockade

When the Soviets finally lifted the blockade, the division of Germany into two states was a reality. West Germany became a democratic pro-American state, while East Germany remained under Communist control.

The geographic and political division of Europe was reinforced by a military division in 1949. Most of the Western European powers and America signed a military alliance called NATO – North Atlantic Treaty Organisation. The Soviet Union set up a similar Eastern Bloc organisation, called the Warsaw Pact, in 1955, when West Germany joined NATO.

In 1949, the Soviet Union caught up with the USA and developed nuclear weapons. By 1952 the Americans had developed the hydrogen bomb, which was many times more destructive than the atom bomb. This time it only took the Soviets nine months to catch up.

Korean War, 1950–53

The first military crisis of the Cold War years was outside Europe, in Korea.

Communist North Korea, possibly with Stalin's encouragement, invaded and conquered American-supported South Korea. America asked the United Nations to support South Korea. The Soviet Union were at this time boycotting the Security Council of the United Nations and thereby missed their opportunity to veto the decision. As the war in Korea between the UN, led by America, and North Korea, supported by Communist China, was fought out, the Soviet Union was left out. The Korean War ended in stalemate with South Korea re-established as a pro-American state and North Korea remaining Communist. America was emerging as the policeman of the world.

The Cold War had made the world a very tense and dangerous place to live.

1   How did the atomic bomb affect the relationship between the USA and the USSR?
2   What, according to Source A, were Churchill and Stalin trying to decide?
3   What did Churchill mean by 'an Iron Curtain' in Source B?
4   How did Stalin reply to Churchill's speech?
5   How do you account for the differences between Sources D and E?
6   Did Truman rule out military action in Source D?
7   Why, in Sources H and I, was there such strong criticism of the Marshall Plan, Source G?
8   What, according to Source F was the purpose of the Marshall Plan?
9   Do you think the Marshall Plan was motivated by generosity or American self-interest?
10 Explain the reasons why Berlin was so important to both the USA and the USSR?
11 How does the term 'Cold War' describe Soviet-American relations after 1945?

Essay: Describe the causes and development of the Cold War, 1945–1955.

11 Khrushchev: A new style

Stalin's legacy

The brutality of the 1930's re-emerged after the Second World War in the Soviet Union. Stalin transplanted the entire population of Tartars from their homes in the Crimea to the centre of the Soviet Union. Large numbers died as they were moved. He also displaced other ethnic peoples whom he believed were not loyal. In turn, many Russians were moved into vulnerable border areas, such as the three Baltic republics, in order to Russify them and make them secure. The Jews were accused of being more interested in Israel than the Soviet Union. Many of their most brilliant leaders were executed. Stalin accused a group of Jewish doctors of plotting to kill him and overthrow the Government. However, in 1953, before this purge could spread like those in the 1930's, Stalin died.

Stalin had ruled the Soviet Union for so long and had so dominated the Government that it was unclear how the country would be run without him. He had helped to win the Civil War. His view of Communism and the world had held sway over Trotsky's – 'Socialism in one country' meant that the Soviet Union had to be built up before Communism was exported. He transformed agriculture by modernizing farming methods but, as in all other aspects of his policies, the human cost was enormous. His main concern was the safety of the Soviet Union and to ensure this he modernized her industries. All opposition, real or imaginary, was wiped out, and millions disappeared into thousands of forced labour camps. When the Germans invaded, Stalin led his country in the war against Hitler and went on to take over Eastern Europe, expanding the Soviet empire to the heart of Europe. His ultimate legacy to the world was a tense, highly-armed and dangerous Cold War. What would his successor(s) do? How would they cope? What type of government would there be?

There was no obvious successor to Stalin, which is not surprising because, as we have seen, Stalin got rid of all his potential opponents. For a couple of years there was a collective leadership. However, soon Nikita Khrushchev emerged as the leader. He was lively and with common sense type views – very much a man of the people. He had had no formal education. He lacked the social airs and graces expected of a national leader. However, he introduced a new, more relaxed climate in the Soviet Union to replace the climate of fear through which Stalin had reigned. When his colleagues in the collective leadership disagreed with him he didn't have them arrested and executed.

De-Stalinization

Khrushchev condemned Stalin in a famous, supposedly secret, speech to the 20th Party Congress in 1956. He criticised many aspects of Stalin's rule. He said that Stalin had taken too much power to himself and had not allowed the Party to rule. He told people about the purges of the 1930's. He told his audience that nuclear war had to be avoided and the way forward was peaceful co-existence with the West. This three hour denunciation of Stalin was one of the most dramatic and significant speeches of the modern era.

Stalin acted not through persuasion, but by imposing his concepts and demanding absolute submission to his opinion. Whoever opposed this concept was doomed to physical annihilation. Mass arrests and deportations of thousands of people, execution without trial, created conditions of insecurity, fear, and even desperation ... Stalin was a very distrustful man, sickly suspicious. He could look at a man and say 'why are your eyes so shifty today?' or 'Why are you turning away so much today and avoiding looking me directly in the eyes?' Everywhere and in everything he saw 'enemies', 'two facers', and 'spies'. Possessing unlimited power he indulged in great wilfulness and choked a person morally and physically. A situation was created where one could not express one's own will ...

And how is it possible that a person confesses to a crime that he has not committed? Only in one way – because of the application of physical methods of pressuring him, tortures, bringing him to a state of unconsciousness, deprivation of his judgment, taking away of his human dignity. In this manner were confessions acquired ...

Stalin had completely lost consciousness of reality; he demonstrated his suspicion and haughtiness not only in relation to individuals in the USSR but in relation to whole parties and nations.

From Khrushchev's secret speech, 1956

Khrushchev's speech had criticized Stalin's abuses of power, his persecution of minorities like the Tartars, and his mistakes in the Second World War.

Khrushchev began a policy of de-Stalinization. The worst excesses of Stalinism were the gulags which Solzhenitsyn had called a gulag archipelago (a chain of labour camp islands). Two years after his speech most of the Siberian labour camps were emptied. The Government destroyed statues and pictures of Stalin and renamed many places that had been named after the former dictator – Stalingrad, the scene of one of the worst battles of the Second World War, was renamed Volgograd. The Chinese Communist leader Mao Tse-tung, who took power in 1949, disagreed with Khrushchev and thought he was wrong to criticize Stalin. Mao fundamentally opposed Khrushchev's policy of peaceful co-existence with the Capitalist countries of the West. Mao insisted that China was the only country that could win a nuclear war because it had such a large population – Khrushchev was alarmed at this. He called the Chinese 'madmen' who could bring about a nuclear war. Khrushchev ended the Soviet assistance to China. The Communist world fell out among themselves. There was now two ways to Communism – the Soviet way and the Chinese way.

Khrushchev wanted to peacefully co-exist with the West but he also wanted to compete with them: 'Let us see who produces more per head of population, who provides a higher material and cultural standard for the people.'

Khrushchev's most far reaching reforms were in agriculture. Most of his time and energy was given to this subject – he made hundreds of speeches about it. Millions of acres of uncultivated land were ploughed up. Khrushchev wanted to solve the problem of the shortage of grain. However, much of the land was unsuitable for grain growing and his virgin land project failed after a few years. The first few years were very successful but soon the topsoil was eroded away and a giant dust bowl was left in Siberia. Khrushchev was keenly embarrassed when he had to import grain from America in 1963 and 1964. Many people felt that he was meddling in farming without knowing enough about it.

Khrushchev also allowed a limited form of democracy with the Communist Party – a small fraction of the Communist Party would be replaced on a regular basis. Even though only a tiny fraction of the population could vote in these Party elections, it was still a step forward from the age of Stalin.

Intervention In Eastern Europe

The first major international crisis that the collective leadership had to face after the death of Stalin in 1953 was an uprising in East Berlin. Harsh living conditions and restrictive policies in East Berlin had led to serious discontent. 50,000 workers rebelled in East Berlin. The uprising quickly spread to other parts of East Germany. East German officials (all loyal Communists) called on the Soviet occupation force to put down the uprising. Soviet forces quickly crushed the uprising. This was to be a recurring theme in post-war history – how was the Soviet Union to keep Eastern Europe as a satellite?

B

A few building workers on one site downed tools refusing to work to the new norms (increased output from the workers demanded by the Government) ... A banner suddenly appeared demanding the abolition of the norms. With this the group began to march down the Stalinallee ... joined on the way by the workers at all the other sites ... it turned into a march on the Government ... they decided on a general strike for the next day ... about 100,000 marched through the streets ... A number attempted to storm the Economics Ministry but were driven back by the rubber truncheons of the police. The rest turned towards the Potsdamerplatz and it was here that the police opened fire. Twenty Russian tanks began to clear the Lustergarten at the same time; tanks then appeared in all parts of the city ... tanks also opened fire on groups of young people who tried to stop them by throwing stones into the tracks ... By nightfall the Soviet army was in complete control.

From *City on Leave* by Philip Windsor, 1953

In Poland in 1956 the expectations of many people were raised by Khrushchev's denunciation of Stalin. They now expected and called for sweeping reforms inside Poland. At the 8th Party Congress in Poland, in 1956, it was proposed that Wladyslaw Gomulka be appointed as Secretary of the Party. This was clearly an attempt to defy Moscow because Gomulka had been dismissed by Stalin in 1949. During the summer of 1956 the people of Warsaw had risen in revolt. The crisis deepened when the soldiers refused to shoot on the strikers. The appointment of Gomulka was an attempt to bring about changes in Poland that would lessen the discontent. Gomulka wanted to make Poland more independent of the Soviet Union. Khrushchev was alarmed at the Polish news. He arrived with other Soviet leaders at the Polish Communist Party Congress and he joined in the discussions.

Soviet tanks advance against demonstrating workers at the Potsdamerplatz in East Berlin in June 1953

The Poles were determined to run their own affairs, but they assured Khrushchev that they would remain as loyal members of the Communist Bloc. Khrushchev reluctantly gave in and accepted a new Polish government under Gomulka. He allowed Gomulka control over Poland's internal affairs. Khrushchev decided against intervention with Soviet troops because this might have led to further nationalist revolts against the Soviet Union throughout Eastern Europe.

▼ C

The 'Thaw' (the easing of tension between Russia and the West) in Russia created expectations of reform in Poland. Communism had not put down deep roots in Poland. Polish agriculture had not been collectivized. The Catholic Church remained very strong, and the deeply patriotic Poles resented the presence of Russian troops on their soil. In June 1956 workers in Poznov went on strike in protest against working conditions. They demanded that Gomulka, who had been expelled from the Communist Party ... be re-admitted to the Party and to the government. The strike movement spread rapidly. Khrushchev put Russian troops in and around Poland on the alert, fearing that the Polish government might lose control of the situation. Then he flew to Warsaw to discuss the crisis with the leaders of the Polish Communist Party. He decided to allow Gomulka to emerge as the new leader of Poland and to purge some of the unpopular Stalinists in the government. Gomulka promised that Poland would remain a loyal member of the Warsaw Pact. Khrushchev calculated that using the Russian army to crush the strike movement would have deepened the Poles' hatred of the Russians and would have created more problems than it solved.

From *Russia: A modern History,* by David Warnes, 1984

This tolerance in Poland, and his visit the previous year to Tito in Yugoslavia, seemed to show that Khrushchev believed in his concept of 'different roads to Socialism'. But his reaction to events in Hungary wasn't so tolerant. The developments in Poland greatly encouraged the Hungarians. The Hungarian Prime Minister, Imre Nagy, declared Hungary a neutral country, which alarmed the Soviets. The Communist Party's monopoly on power was ended and opposition parties were to be allowed. Nagy wanted Hungary to be released from the Warsaw Pact. If he accepted this, Khrushchev would, he felt, be accepting the end of the Communist Bloc in Eastern Europe. Soviet forces acted swiftly and brutally put down the Hungarian experiment with independence. There was little that could be done against 6,000 tanks. 3,000 Hungarians were killed in a few days and the Red Army controlled Hungary. The people of Hungary called out to the West for help; they had believed the American Secretary of State, Dulles, when he promised to 'liberate people from Communism'. However, the Americans were not willing to intervene in the Soviet zone, fearing that it would lead to a nuclear war.

Hungarians gather around a statue of Stalin which has been toppled over by protestors in Budapest

▼

 is at cx 0.69

D

It all began on 23rd October 1956 with a demonstration at the statue of a national hero, Bena. Fifty thousand people sang the national anthem, and then fifty thousand people started to cry; students, grown men and officers … they were not ashamed of their tears. A resolution was read out 'We want an independent national policy. Our relations with all countries and with the USSR should be on the basis of the principle of equality'.

From *An Hungarian born writer*, by George Mikas

E

From the Russian point of view the situation had got entirely out of control. It represented a dual threat to Soviet domination of Eastern Europe. The movement had to be nipped in the bud before it could flower.
On the 4th of November the Soviet army moved into Budapest to impose Soviet military control. Upwards of twenty thousand Hungarians were killed and ten times that number fled to the West. The leaders of the Revolution, including Nagy, were subsequently shot, and a pro-Soviet government headed by Kadar was established by the Soviet military authorities.

From *Eastern Europe 1956–78,* by Christopher Donnelly, 1978

In 1948 the Soviets had backed down over Berlin and let supplies through after a ten month siege. In 1956 it was the Americans who backed down. Even though the Americans had led the Hungarians to believe that they would support them, no help came. It was clear that Khrushchev was not going to give up Soviet control of Eastern Europe. The Revolution in Hungary was seen by the Soviets as going too far. The Hungarians had tried to test how far de-Stalinization could go. Khrushchev was clearly intent on holding the Eastern Bloc together and not allowing any independence that might lead to a break away from Moscow.

Some of the Hungarian citizens killed by the Soviet army when it put down the 1956 uprising

Peaceful co-existence

Khrushchev realised that the nuclear age was forcing the superpowers to change how they behaved towards each other. The Soviet Union was the first to develop the technology to send nuclear bombs as missiles half way around the world. Both sides were stockpiling weapons of awful destructive force. This mutual balance of terror made nuclear war, or any war that led to nuclear war, unthinkable. This mutual assured destruction (MAD) made Khrushchev realise that Communism could not be spread by military means. He coined the phrase peaceful co-existence to describe how the superpowers should live alongside each other. He wanted to settle disputes through discussion, not through war: 'there must' he said 'be peaceful co-existence or the most destructive war in history, there is no third way'.

However, Khrushchev was full of contradictions. Even though he talked of disarmament he promised to turn out missiles like sausages. He also continued with the goal of worldwide Communism. He competed with the Americans for friends and allies in Africa, Asia, and Latin America, but he was careful in his support for wars of liberation not to antagonize the Americans too much.

When West Germany was admitted into the West's defence group, NATO, Khrushchev responded by setting up a mutual defence group for all the Eastern European states – the Warsaw Pact. He also continued the build up of nuclear weapons. Each country developed intercontinental ballistic missiles (ICBMs) – these rockets could quickly travel from one superpower to the other. Both sides were afraid that the other would develop better weapons and use this superiority to threaten and dominate the other. Khrushchev stole a march on the Americans by sending the first space satellite into orbit. The West became more fearful as it seemed that the Soviets were overtaking them in the nuclear race. The race for nuclear advantage and space

exploration went ahead apace, with the Soviets often getting some spectacular firsts.

The relations between America and the Soviet Union had improved a little under Khrushchev until it was discovered in 1960 that the Americans were spying on the Soviet Union. The Soviet Union shot down an American U2 spy plane. The U2 incident worsened relations between the two superpowers. China had always been critical of Khrushchev's idea of peaceful co-existence. They argued that this spying incident proved the Americans could not be trusted.

The Soviet Union sent the first animal into space. This photograph shows Laika, the Russian space dog, in her capsule in Sputnik II before take off. Unfortunately, the Soviet scientists had not yet developed a way of bringing the capsule back again!

This Soviet cartoon from 1960 shows the American President, Eisenhower, attempting to disguise a U2 spy plane as a dove of peace

Berlin again

Tension was increased even more in 1961 over Berlin. Ever since the Berlin blockade and airlift, the crisis over the future of Berlin had deepened. West Berlin had grown more and more prosperous. Marshall Aid meant that the standard of living in West Berlin was far greater than that of East Berlin.

▼ F

Our presence in West Berlin cannot be ended by any act of the Soviet government. The NATO shield was long ago extended to cover West Berlin ... For West Berlin, lying exposed 110 miles inside East Germany surrounded by Soviet troops and close to Soviet supply lines, has many roles. It is more than a showcase of liberty, a symbol, an island of freedom in a Communist sea. It is even more than a link with the free world; a beacon of hope behind the iron curtain; an escape hatch for refugees.
It is the great testing place of Western courage and will, a focal point where solemn commitments and Soviet ambitions now meet in basic confrontation.

President Kennedy speaking in July 1961. This summed up the attitude of America towards Berlin.

The people of East Berlin began to vote with their feet, they left East Berlin in their thousands for a better life in the West. At one stage 10,000 people a week were defecting to the West. The economy of East Berlin could not take this human haemorrhage. Many of the escapees were the best educated and most talented people in the city – the doctors, teachers, and technicians. To stop this embarrassing flood, the Soviets cut off the city, initially with barbed wire and then with walls of concrete. The Berlin Wall cut off the East from the West, families, friends, and neighbours were cut off from each other.

The Soviet Bloc was firmly cut off from the West. Those who tried to cross the Wall were shot. In fact over 40 people were shot trying to escape to the West in the first year. Even though the West was apparently very angry about the Wall, they were unwilling to take any action. Kennedy, the American President, said 'If they wanted to attack us they wouldn't be putting up barbed wire borders. I'm not going to get het up about it'.

▲
A West Berliner standing on his car to wave to friends in East Berlin over the newly built Berlin Wall in 1961. The Wall was later built much higher.

◄
East German border guards remove the body of nineteen-year-old Peter Fechter, who was shot trying to escape over the Berlin Wall in September 1962

Cuban missile crisis

The situation remained tense between the two superpowers until 1962, when they went perilously close to the brink of war. A frightened world stood by as the superpowers threatened each other over Cuba. One of the American spy planes discovered something very serious in Cuba – Russian nuclear missile sites.

Cuba is very close to America and had been under American influence. It had been run by a right wing dictator, called Batista, who was overthrown in 1959 by Fidel Castro, a Marxist revolutionary. America, in turn, unsuccessfully tried to overthrow Castro in a failed invasion. Castro turned to the Soviet Union for support and the Soviets began to set up secret missile sites on the coast of Cuba facing the USA. America could not tolerate Soviet nuclear missile sites on its doorstep. This would have allowed the Soviet Union to break through the whole complex set of alliances that America had developed to contain Communism (NATO in Western Europe and SEATO in South East Asia). Missiles in Cuba could easily reach all of America's main cities.

On 22nd October President Kennedy announced that he was setting up a naval blockade of Cuba. He insisted that Khrushchev withdraw the missiles and move back from the brink of the abyss. The Soviet ships sailing towards Cuba were destined to be met by the blockade. The world held its breath as this ultimate brinkmanship of the Cold War was acted out.

As the ships approached the blockade they slowed down. Khrushchev told Kennedy that he would dismantle the sites if America lifted the blockade and promised not to attack Cuba. Kennedy accepted. To the Americans they were eyeball to eyeball and the Soviets blinked. To most observers this was a real victory for the Americans and a humiliating climb down for Khrushchev. When the crisis passed, the missile sites were dismantled and the missiles were sent back to the Soviet Union.

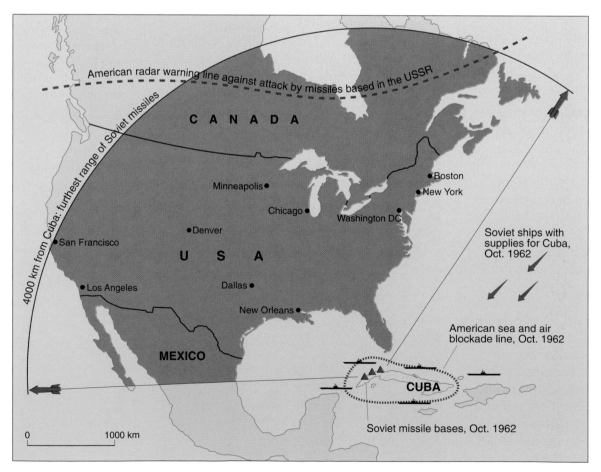

◀ The range of Soviet missiles based in Cuba

However, the crisis made both sides realise that they had to avoid such tension again. A direct phone link (a hot line) was set up between the White House and the Kremlin. While they agreed to direct phone links the Soviets also planned increased military spending so they would not be outdone by the American nuclear superiority again.

The Cuban Missile Crisis was a personal disaster for Khrushchev. America had won the war of nerves. The hardliners in the Kremlin would not forgive Khrushchev for this embarrassing set back. The Communist Party had regained ultimate control after Stalin's death. In 1964, the Central Committee of the Party removed Khrushchev from power.

Khrushchev: an assessment

The frightening arbitrary brutality of the Stalinist era was eased under Khrushchev. The worst excesses of the law were changed – for example, you could no longer be charged with being a relative of a convicted person.

Writers and intellectuals welcomed the new, more relaxed regime. With the death of Stalin, writers were now asked to reflect reality. Those who were previously banned were now permitted. Khrushchev wanted all his government to read the harrowing account of life in the gulags in the novel *One Day in the Life of Ivan Denisovich* by Alexander Solzhenitsyn. This book was published in 1962 and was a damning criticism of Stalin's labour camps. The practice of imprisoning and exiling writers was ended under Khrushchev. But it was a limited freedom and many were still criticized for their work. Khrushchev encouraged the writers to decide for themselves if a work should be published or not. A work was likely to be published if it criticized Stalin.

The freedom of the press was still limited, as were some subjects for writers. Boris Pasternak was not allowed to publish his novel *Doctor Zhivago* in the Soviet Union because it dealt with the Revolution and the Civil War. Writers could criticize Stalin and his labour camps, but not the Revolution. *Doctor Zhivago* was, however, published abroad in 1957. Pasternak was awarded the Nobel Prize for Literature in 1958.

This new, partial, freedom of expression was very important in the Soviet Union, where the people are well read; and new poetry became very popular among the young. Writers very often had the young in mind, hoping that they would be influenced by their ideas and then change the future Soviet Union.

Khrushchev was no lover of modern art. He once looked at a painting of a lemon in an art gallery and observed loudly that 'it's messy lines which look as if some child has done his business on the canvas'.

Khrushchev began his inspection in the room in which paintings by Bilyutin and some friends of mine had been hung. He swore horribly and became extremely angry about them. It was there that he said that a donkey could do better with his tail.

From *Khrushchev,* by Medvedev, 1982

On another occasion he said that ballet dancers were indecently dressed girls in petticoats. But he also criticized Stalin's policy of not allowing many artists such as ballet dancers to travel abroad in case they defected to the West.

Khrushchev followed a moderate policy towards the non-Russian people of the

Soviet Union. He began by believing, like Lenin, that the people could be drawn together. National languages would be allowed to develop as long as this did not reinforce barriers between people. At the same time, he insisted that everyone become fluent in Russian, which was to be taught at every level across the Union.

However, around 1960, a new wave of persecution and repression began, largely because religion was proving to be so popular. Monasteries were closed and the number of churches fell back to 7,500. The State refused to replace older priests (priests had to be formally registered). When their churches were closed, believers were not allowed to worship together in each other's houses. Many responded by setting up house churches; the authorities replied with imprisonment. The plight of the believers in Russia became a cause for concern in Western countries, who began to watch the situation carefully. Religious freedom in the Soviet Union was to become an issue of human rights in the 1970's and 1980's.

Under Khrushchev, working conditions rose and living standards improved as more consumer goods were available in the shops. Pensions and other social welfare benefits were substantially increased. Large scale building work was undertaken to create more houses and to build some spectacular public buildings like the Lenin Stadium, which was the largest sports stadium in the world. Khrushchev also improved the quality of education in the Soviet Union – more schools and colleges were built and the numbers at university tripled. With the space research programme being so important, much emphasis was placed on the teaching of

The Soviet monument to the space conquerors in Moscow

▼

science and technology – the Soviet Union sent the first satellite into space in 1957 and the first man into space in 1961.

However, Khrushchev's successes have to be considered alongside his failures. He had tried to solve the country's agricultural problems. He amalgamated the collective farms into gigantic units, like farm cities. Previously uncultivated virgin lands were ploughed up and even fallow land was put to the plough in a single-minded drive to increase food production. It was successful initially. But it was quite unscientific: not enough pesticides and fertilizers were used. Whole areas suffered terrible soil erosion. The topsoil was left unprotected and the wind stripped millions of tons away. Six million hectares of land were lost completely.

Much of the grain was also sown in areas which were unsuitable. The result was a shortage of food – food riots took place in some areas and had to be put down by force. Eventually food rationing had to be introduced. Likewise in industry, production fell during the Khrushchev years which led to shortages in the shops. This added to the general discontent.

Khrushchev faced mounting criticism. Some of his critics were old Stalinists who were opposed to his attempts to de-Stalinize the country. They felt that he was unjust in his attitude towards Stalin's wartime achievements. His behaviour at the United Nations in 1960, when he took off his shoe and banged the table to get attention, also caused great embarrassment. His experimentation with agriculture was regarded as harebrained. But, ultimately, he lost the confidence of the powerful in the Soviet Union over his defeat in Cuba. He was called back from holiday in October 1964 to be told that neither the government or the Central Committee had any confidence in him. He had to resign. *Pravda* said 'Harebrained scheming, hasty conclusions, rash decisions based on wishful thinking, boasting, and empty words … all these are defects alien to the Party'.

Khrushchev was the acceptable human face of Communism. He was different to

Stalin in so many ways: he was outgoing, one of the people, out spoken. He wanted to improve the standard of living of the ordinary people. While he continued to stockpile a frightening array of nuclear weapons, he advocated a policy of peaceful co-existence. However, his policies split the Communist world. His biographer said that: 'He left his country a better place than he found it'. He had changed the way of doing things in the Soviet Union. When the Central Committee ousted him they did not use the Stalin way of crudely stage-managed trials or mysteriously falling out of upstairs windows – Khrushchev was outmanoeuvred politically.

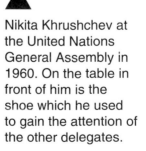

Nikita Khrushchev at the United Nations General Assembly in 1960. On the table in front of him is the shoe which he used to gain the attention of the other delegates.

▲

Khrushchev standing in the middle of a cornfield in the new cultivated virgin lands

1 Why did Khrushchev make his 'secret speech'?

2 What was 'de-Stalinization'?

3 Why do you think Khrushchev thought it was so important to keep control over Eastern Europe?

4 What might have happened if the East German uprising had succeeded?

5 What did the demonstrators in Source D mean by their resolution?

6 Write a brief justification that the USSR might have given for crushing the Hungarian uprising.

7 The USA was horrified by the events in Hungary. Explain their reaction.

8 Was there an 'arms race' during the 1950s?

9 What effect do you think the atomic bomb had on Soviet-American relations during the 1950s?

10 What purpose did Kennedy have in making his speech, Source F?

11 What arguments were put forward for and against the building of the Berlin Wall?

12 Was Kennedy right to be worried about missiles in Cuba?

13 i) Why did Khrushchev remove the missiles from Cuba?
ii) What might have happened if he had refused?

Essay: Khrushchev died in 1971. He had not been mentioned in the Soviet press since 1964. Write an obituary describing his successes and failures as leader of the USSR.

12 *Brezhnev to Chernenko: the old guard*

After Khrushchev was ousted he was replaced by a collective leadership. Leonid Brezhnev was soon to emerge as the most important leader. His eighteen years in office were dominated by foreign affairs. He did little to solve the country's economic problems, either in industry or in agriculture. In fact harvests were so poor that grain had to be imported from America.

Unlike Khrushchev, Brezhnev was a conservative, predictable ruler who did not favour reform. He was suspicious of any reform either at home or in the Eastern Bloc. Two novelists, Daniel and Sinyavsky, were put on trial in 1966 for sending their work abroad to be published. However, even though freedom of artistic expression was not allowed, the ordinary citizen did not live in terror as they had done under Stalin. His invasion of Czechoslovakia showed his opposition to any reform in the satellite states.

Things were always uncertain under Khrushchev – he was likely to call a sudden press conference or make some outlandish remark in an art gallery. There was no such uncertainty with Brezhnev. Very few independent-minded authors were allowed to be published. Despite these restrictions, books such as Solzhenitsyn's *The Gulag Archipelago* were published abroad. An underground network developed called Samizdat where work was published and then copies passed around illegally. The Baptists secretly published and distributed about half a million Bibles in 15 years.

In art, the State returned to the expectations of the 1930's – artists were expected to produce socially-relevant work. An experimental exhibition which ignored this social realism was broken up by the police. However, the police did not bother with those who were enjoying such experimental literature and art in the privacy of their own homes.

The restriction in art and literature came at a time when educational achievement was increasing, and this meant a wider demand for more and new ideas. This was a tide that Brezhnev could not hold back. The Soviet Union was no longer a backward illiterate society, but highly educated. Western culture was spread through videos and tapes. The demand for Western freedoms was to grow.

Brezhnev intended to eliminate all differences between the nationalities. He dismissed the politicians who had been encouraging Ukrainian identity and replaced them with Russians. This led to an underground dissident movement in the Ukraine dedicated to the fostering of their own culture. Brezhnev's decision to end the guarantee to keep the national languages alive led to riots in Georgia. Many saw an extension of the influence of Russian, and

A smiling Nikita Khrushchev gives a thumbs down answer to a reporter's question at an informal press conference at the Soviet Embassy in New York in 1960. He was in New York to speak to the United Nations General Assembly.

▼

a threat to their own language, with the introduction of Russian into the nursery schools. Russians increased their influence in all the senior positions. One reason for this was that all advanced education was in Russian.

Czechoslovakia

In 1968, Dubcek, the leader of Czechoslovakia, tried to bring in reforms. He wanted to give Socialism a human face and to ensure that people had more consumer goods (such as cars and radios). The Soviet government did not object to these reforms and, as the changes were popular in Czechoslovakia, Dubcek pressed ahead with further reforms. He intended to allow freedom of the press and freedom of religion; to hold free elections; and to allow other political parties. The Soviet Union now felt that he was going too far and saw these reforms as a serious threat to their whole structure in Eastern Europe. They condemned the reforms as creeping counter-revolution. In effect they were afraid that a Western-style government and economy would emerge. They resolved to end the reforms and the perceived danger. 500,000 Warsaw Pact troops were sent in to put down the reforms. Dubcek, the symbol of the 'Prague Spring', was brought to Moscow. On his return home to Czechoslovakia he announced that Soviet troops would stay, censorship would return and that the period of reform was over. Dubcek was overthrown and a man loyal to Moscow was appointed. As in Hungary, the new government worked under strict supervision from Moscow. Once again the Americans stood back and did not intervene.

A protestor stands in front of a Soviet tank in Prague in 1968

Poland

Brezhnev, said that invasion was justified if the Soviet character of any of the satellite states was threatened. This Brezhnev Doctrine meant that different roads to Socialism did not mean a road away from Moscow. However, his response to demands for reform in Poland was more flexible. In 1980 the situation in Poland was uneasy. The economy was in ruins, and rising prices, food shortages and industrial unrest led to general strikes in the cities. The strikes were led by the shipyard workers in Gdansk. The strikers demanded a free trade union and they won that critical demand. Solidarity (the name of the union) was the first truly independent political movement in Eastern Europe since the war. Solidarity (under the leadership of Lech Walesa) increased their demands and put pressure on the Government to relax censorship and to allow more religious freedom. They demanded free elections with a choice of free political parties.

Even though the Soviets were alarmed at these developments, they felt that sending the troops into Poland where Communism was so unpopular and religion and nationalism so strong would lead to a bloodbath. They tried to intimidate the Poles with large scale army movements along the border, but they did not invade. Instead, they left it to the local leader, General Jaruzelski, to impose martial law.

Solidarity remained active as an underground movement despite the jailing of Walesa and the other leaders. Walesa was awarded the Nobel peace prize in 1983. Mikhail Gorbachev's spirit of reform was widely welcomed in Poland. In 1989, Solidarity candidates won most of the seats in the parliamentary elections, and Walesa was elected the country's President.

Détente

Brezhnev wanted to extend Khrushchev's policy of peaceful co-existence with the West. This policy came to be called détente, which means a permanent relaxation of tension. The Soviet Union wanted détente for a number of reasons. Since the Sino-Soviet split, America and China had been improving their relations. The Soviet Union did not want to be isolated, facing a possible Chinese-American, anti-Soviet alliance. Relations with China remained tense (over border disputes, the disputed leadership of the Communist world, and how to achieve world Socialism) but attempts were made to improve relations with America. It was hoped that this would lead to reduced spending on defence and allow more trade with the West, thereby improving the Soviet economy which was in a chronic state. Both superpowers realised that there was a limit to their power: the Soviet Union realised this over Cuba and America in Vietnam. It was all too clear that the nuclear arms race created intense dangers. Their two leaders met to discuss proposals to reduce tension. Nixon, the American President, visited Moscow in 1972 and

Brezhnev went to Washington in 1973. Nixon was to return to Moscow in 1974.

Nixon and Brezhnev meeting in Moscow in 1974

B

We should recognise that great nuclear powers have a solemn responsibility to exercise restraint in any crisis, and to take positive action to avert direct confrontation ... We should recognise further that it is the responsibility of the great powers to influence other nations in conflict or crisis to moderate their behaviour.

Nixon commenting at the Moscow meeting, 1972

They agreed to try their hardest to avoid military confrontation. Nixon, the first American President to visit the Soviet Union, said in a television address to the Soviet people that if the arms race went unchecked there would be no winners only losers. Together with agreements to try to prevent nuclear war and to work for friendship, they agreed to share scientific research and to increase trade. In a very symbolic gesture American astronauts and Soviet cosmonauts met in space.

The flight was of historic significance as a symbol of the present process of easing the international tension and the improvement of US-Soviet relations on the basis of peaceful co-existence. It was a practical contribution between the USA and USSR in the interests of the peoples of both countries and in the interests of world peace.

Brezhnev's view of the space link up

Helsinki

The most important of the agreements came in 1975 in Helsinki, where both sides agreed to current European borders and ensuring human rights and fundamental freedoms. For the Soviets they had secured the long overdue recognition of Eastern Europe by the West. To the West this was an attempt to ensure human rights – freedom of expression, freedom of religion, and freedom of movement – for the peoples of the Eastern Bloc. The Soviets had continued to flagrantly disregard human rights – Solzhenitsyn was exiled from the Soviet Union and had his passport taken away for publishing *The Gulag Archipelago* in Paris, because it exposed the conditions in the labour camps. After the Helsinki agreement, groups grew up in the Soviet Union and in Eastern Europe campaigning for the promised human rights. They were harassed and imprisoned by the police. America strongly denounced the Soviet treatment of these dissidents.

Afghanistan

A second round of talks began in 1974 but ran into trouble and was not signed until 1979. Then the Americans refused to ratify the agreements because they were outraged by the Soviet invasion of Afghanistan on Christmas Day 1979.

Afghanistan was strategically very important to the Soviet Union. The Soviets wanted to counter the growing American influence in Pakistan next door. Brezhnev also feared that Afghanistan might become a fundamentalist Islamic state like Iran. He was anxious to avoid an Islamic circle of states on his southern border and he feared how his own Islamic people (a sizable minority in the Soviet Union) might react to the example of Islamic states breaking away from Soviet influence.

Brezhnev told Carter, the American President, that he had been invited to invade by the Afghan government and they would soon leave. Carter was furious.

Afghan Mujahideen fighters praying towards Mecca before going into battle with the Soviet army

This action has made a more dramatic change in my own opinion of what the Soviets' ultimate goals are than anything they have done.

President Carter's opinion of the Soviet invasion of Afghanistan

To the West it seemed that the Soviets were using old fashioned military tactics to increase their influence. America responded with a boycott of the Moscow Olympic Games. They also imposed economic sanctions on the Soviet Union and sent aid to the Afghan rebels. Carter went on to proclaim that the Persian Gulf region was of vital interest to the USA and would be protected by military force if necessary. The invasion put an end to détente and the old Cold War tensions returned.

Leonid Brezhnev being helped to his seat after giving a speech in 1979. By this time, his health was failing him.

Brezhnev had been in poor health for years and the country was allowed to drift. There was very little change, new ideas were not welcome. With such stagnation at the top, many ordinary citizens began to demand reform, often at great personal risk to themselves. They spread their radical ideas by an underground newspaper which was passed from member to member. When Brezhnev died there was still no sign of reform. His two elderly successors, Andropov and Chernenko, continued Brezhnev's cautious conservative policies. Those demanding reform had to wait until 1985 when Mikhail Gorbachev came to power.

1   Why was 'Samizdat' necessary?
2   Why couldn't the USSR have left Dubcek and Czechoslovakia to decide their own affairs?
3   What effect would the Soviet intervention in Czechoslovakia have had on their relations with the USA?
4   Would Source A have been published in the USSR?
5   Describe the possible feelings of the man in Source A and those of the Russian tank driver.
6   Do you think most Russians supported their country's interference in Eastern European countries?
7   How do Sources B and C support the idea of détente?
8   Why did President Carter's opinion about the USSR change in Source D.
9   Do you think Soviet behaviour contradicted the principles of the Helsinki agreement?
10 In protest over Soviet policy the USA boycotted the 1980 Olympic Games. Should sports events be used by politicians in this way?

Essay: How successful was Leonid Brezhnev in improving Soviet-American relations?

13 *A* new Russia

Gorbachev

The ten years after Gorbachev came to power saw another revolution in Russia, during which the Soviet Union was transformed.

Gorbachev's first official announcement was to praise détente and to call for a reduction in arms. He wanted to meet Reagan, the current American President, as soon as possible. To the West he seemed like a breath of fresh air: open minded and committed to reform. To Margaret Thatcher, the British Prime Minister, he was a man she could do business with.

A

Mr Gorbachev is a magnetic figure who has caught the imagination of the world. The world has responded by sending camera crews of correspondents in their hundreds to scrutinize his country, now more open to such inspection than at any time in its history.

Rupert Cornwell describes Gorbachev's attraction in The Independent, 16th November 1987

Gorbachev mania in Germany in 1989

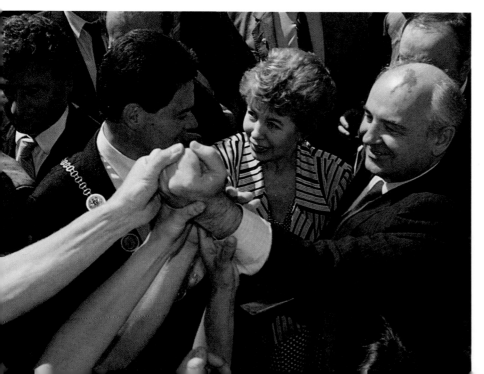

Gorbachev's policies of Glasnost and Perestroika brought root and branch changes to the Soviet Union.

Glasnost

Glasnost (the Russian word for openness) meant that there was more freedom. Gorbachev allowed more freedom of expression in books and in the media generally; journalists were allowed to print real news and in a critical fashion. Artists were allowed to experiment in music and in films. *Pravda* (the Party newspaper) printed an article very critical of how Brezhnev treated the dissidents. Gorbachev ended the appalling practice of Andropov and Brezhnev of locking dissidents away in mental hospitals. In 1986 Dr Andrei Sakharov, the father figure of Soviet dissidents, was released from internal exile. Gorbachev phoned him with the news that he would be welcome to return. The following year he pardoned 150 dissidents. The media at home and abroad were delighted with the greatly increased access to information. Mrs Thatcher was given a warm welcome when she went walkabout in Moscow. An air of normality was returning to the country.

Perestroika

His policy of Perestroika (the Russian word for restructuring) was an attempt to reorganise and reform the economy, which was in danger of complete collapse. Workers were allowed to set up co-operatives and small family businesses were encouraged. This encouragement of free enterprise and market forces was a radical shift from the past and an attempt to improve competition and increase employment. The basic Communist economic philosophy of State control was being challenged and changed.

B ▼

If you want to find the real culture of Perestroika, to understand the main pastime of young Moscow, you have to hear rock music which the State has at last begun to encourage. It is now acceptable.

The problem of all this activity in the Soviet Union is that it is all being authorised from the top, agreed to by the man in the Kremlin, Gorbachev. The whole Perestroika and Glasnost did not spring from below. It took a political decision from the man at the top; if you like 'a liberal Tsar', Gorbachev.

The question really is what happens after Gorbachev goes and how long has he got?

From a Granada television programme about the changes in Gorbachev's USSR

Gorbachev also began to reorganise the political system by introducing elections for local government. This was an attempt to give up central control of the people in exchange for freedom and prosperity. These policies caught the imagination of the press across the world. Gorbachev transformed the Soviet Union by liberalizing the oppressive strict censorship of his predecessors. Thought control was abandoned and the State tolerated open news and criticism. Artists were to be allowed to express a wide range of opinions and historians were to write the truth about the past. *Izvestia* admitted that the official textbooks were full of lies. There was great excitement at the freedom to read a wide variety of books previously banned. What was previously taboo became commonplace on television.

 C ▼

At the end of the last twelve months the Soviet Union is a different place thanks to him. And in the world beyond Russia he has been the prime instigator of change.

His initiative has led to the first arms treaty to reduce nuclear stockpiles.

But much more important, is the change in attitude towards his country that Gorbachev has brought in the minds of the people in the West. Who would have imagined a year ago that a book written by a Kremlin leader would be a best seller in the Capitalist world?

At home the changes are even more remarkable. Compared with just one year ago Russians can now think more freely almost without fear of reprisal. They can emigrate in increasing – though still small – numbers. Seeing and reading certain plays, films, and novels once banned is no longer dangerous. However, some foreign radio stations are still jammed ... Despite the release of two hundred and seventy-five political prisoners, many others still remain in the gulags.

From *The Sunday Times,* 27th December 1987

Reduction of Nuclear Missiles

He also tried to make the world a safer place by reducing nuclear weapons. He began by stopping any new missiles being stationed in Eastern Europe. At his first meeting with President Reagan in Geneva, both sides agreed to work for a cut in nuclear arsenals. Gorbachev said he wanted a 15 year timetable to rid the earth gradually of nuclear weapons. There was also agreement on humanitarian issues, such as allowing Jews to emigrate from the Soviet Union. After the Summit, he gave the press an unprecedented 90 minute interview in which he said that this was a positive start and the world had become a safer place. The two leaders met again at Reykjavik in Iceland in October 1986. Gorbachev proposed further cuts, but this depended on America giving up its Star Wars plan (Strategic Defence Initiative, a programme to destroy missiles in flight). The Americans refused to give up Star Wars and so progress was slowed down. Yet in the following year the two superpower leaders agreed that all intermediate range missiles were to be destroyed over the next three years. A significant start had been made to the reduction of nuclear weapons. Gorbachev also wanted to reduce the Soviet Union's huge land forces by 500,000 men. In 1990 he agreed to a huge reduction in his conventional (non-nuclear) forces based in Europe.

Afghanistan was turning out to be the Soviet Union's Vietnam, with huge forces caught up there at great cost in a war they could not win against the local guerrilla forces. The occupation and war had brought worldwide criticism. Gorbachev began to pull out the Soviet forces in May 1988.

Despite his successes and the undoubted change in the Soviet Union, there were serious problems. In 1986 the nuclear reactor in the power station at Chernobyl caught fire. High levels of radioactive emissions spread across the Soviet Union, Scandinavia, and Northern Europe. Even though Glasnost allowed the media to thoroughly investigate the disaster, the world could now see how out of date the Soviet economy had become. His reforms had not brought about the promised improved living standards, in fact quite the reverse – the already ailing economy was getting worse.

Mikhail Gorbachev in New York with President Reagan and Vice President Bush in 1988